Multicultural Math Fun

Holidays Around the Year

Louise Bock, Susan Guengerich, and Hope Martin

illustrated by Margery Niblock

J. WESTON
WALCH
PUBLISHER
PORTLAND, MAINE

User's Guide
to
Walch Reproducible Books

As part of our general effort to provide educational materials which are as practical and economical as possible, we have designated this publication a "reproducible book." The designation means that purchase of the book includes purchase of the right to limited reproduction of all pages on which this symbol appears:

Here is the basic Walch policy: We grant to individual purchasers of this book the right to make sufficient copies of reproducible pages for use by all students of a single teacher. This permission is limited to a single teacher, and does not apply to entire schools or school systems, so institutions purchasing the book should pass the permission on to a single teacher. Copying of the book or its parts for resale is prohibited.

Any questions regarding this policy or requests to purchase further reproduction rights should be addressed to:

Permissions Editor
J. Weston Walch, Publisher
321 Valley Street • P. O. Box 658
Portland, Maine 04104-0658

1   2   3   4   5   6   7   8   9   10
ISBN 0-8251-2905-2
Copyright © 1997
J. Weston Walch, Publisher
P.O. Box 658 • Portland, Maine 04104-0658
Printed in the United States of America

▼ ▼ ▼ ▼ ▼ ▼ ▼ ▼ ▼ ▼ ▼ ▼ ▼ ▼ ▼ ▼ ▼

Contents

▼ ▼ ▼ ▼ ▼ ▼ ▼ ▼ ▼ ▼ ▼ ▼ ▼ ▼ ▼ ▼ ▼

▼ ▼ ▼ ▼ ▼ ▼ ▼ ▼ ▼ ▼ ▼ ▼ ▼ ▼ ▼ ▼ ▼ ▼ ▼

To the Teacher

▼ ▼ ▼ ▼ ▼ ▼ ▼ ▼ ▼ ▼ ▼ ▼ ▼ ▼ ▼ ▼ ▼ ▼ ▼

The activities and projects in *Multicultural Math Fun: Holidays Around the Year* are designed to enhance mathematics with multicultural celebrations of holidays and special events throughout the year.

The National Council of Teachers of Mathematics (NCTM) standards have served as our inspiration to help you make the mathematics of your curriculum a celebration. We modeled our celebrations after the first four standards—Mathematics as Problem Solving, Mathematics as Communication, Mathematics as Reasoning, and Mathematical Connections. These standards are echoed in each of the activities and projects. Many of the activities are designed to be completed in cooperative learning groups, encouraging students to communicate mathematically. Alternatives to traditional assessments, including journal topics, are provided.

Most of the activities or projects are accompanied by a teacher page. A brief description of the information and suggestions on the teacher page follows.

Areas of study	This section lists the mathematical skills addressed in the activity. This listing will enable you to connect each activity with strands within your curriculum.
Concepts	This section delineates the mathematical concepts in terms of student learning goals. Assessment criteria should be tied to these conceptual goals.
Materials needed	A detailed list of commonly available, everyday materials is provided to help with organization of the activity. It is best to have these materials on hand in order to facilitate a productive learning environment.
Procedures	This section is not meant to be a step-by-step set of instructions. Rather, it is a guide or brief overview of the total lesson. This approach to procedures will allow you the freedom to use your own unique teaching style.

Assessment   There are normally three areas listed under Assessment. They are:

1. Student products: Did the students complete the work properly? Is their computation correct? Did they understand what they were doing?

2. Observation of students: If they were working in groups, did they all contribute? Did they cooperate? Did they have unique solutions or use interesting strategies?

3. Journal questions: Writing in the math classroom encourages mathematical communication skills, as highlighted in the NCTM standards. Many of the teacher pages suggest questions for students to answer in writing. Several of the worksheets require students to provide written explanations, as well.

Extension   Extensions are provided for many activities. You are encouraged to use extensions that would further connect these activities to your own curriculum.

Students will need to use a variety of skills to complete these real-life lessons. As they solve real problems, they will focus on more than one skill or concept. Many of the activities cross over skill areas, allowing students to learn skills while solving the problem. This is an integrated approach that enhances concept development.

A brief description of each of the celebrations and their multicultural links is provided at the beginning of each month. Answers to problems with specific solutions can be found at the back of the book. Celebrate and enjoy mathematics throughout the year!

September Celebrations

Introduction

September has been designated as Women of Achievement Month—and so our celebrations in September begin by recognizing two outstanding women mathematicians, Fanya Montalvo and Mary Somerville. Montalvo was born in Monterrey, Mexico. As a young child, she moved to the inner city of Chicago, where she struggled because of her poor English skills, but went on to earn a doctoral degree in mathematical psychology. Born in a small village in Scotland, Somerville was warned that she might go mad if she studied too hard; but she pursued her love of mathematics and earned many honors.

Agatha Christie's Birthday is September 15 (1891). What better way to recognize a woman of achievement than by wishing her a happy birthday. The creator of hundreds of mystery stories, Agatha Christie would have enjoyed the three mystery problems that call for logical thinking.

On September 16, the Mexican people celebrate Mexican Independence Day. A national holiday should be celebrated with entertainment and feasts. The Mexican Independence Day Feast activity contains authentic Mexican recipes. After students make the mathematical conversions for each recipe, they could try preparing the food.

The last Friday in September has been designated as National Native American Day. Native Americans in the Northwest believed in the legendary Sasquatch. The activity The Legend of Bigfoot allows students to approximate the area of their feet while they contemplate the enormous size of Sasquatch's foot. Measurement is the principal mathematics connection in the last Native American celebration when we make Indian fry bread, good for body and soul.

Fanya Montalvo

(1947–)

Born in Monterrey, Mexico, Fanya Montalvo moved to the Logan Square section of Chicago when she was six years old. Her family spoke Spanish at home and she learned English on her own at school. Numbers were the same in Spanish and English, and so mathematics was easier than other subjects for her. Problem solving was fun.

Fanya faced many problems in school. Because her English was poor, she was placed in remedial classes. However, she was very bright. She attended Loyola University in Chicago, majoring in physics. She switched her major to psychology because "the physics department was too cold." Because of her love of mathematics, she chose mathematical psychology, or the study of psychological testing.

Montalvo earned a doctoral degree and began work on artificial intelligence and computer graphics. Speaking of her position, she said, "I feel like I'm on the cutting edge of science. Building intelligent machines is the next step in computer science."

By solving the problems below, you will learn some fascinating facts about machines and computers.

Supercomputer

The fastest and most powerful computer is the liquid-cooled Cray 2, which has a main memory capacity of 32 million bytes.

If all the people in China could make a calculation in a second, it would take the entire population to keep up with this computer.

1. The fastest official record for typing is 216 words per minute. How many words is that per second? _____

2. An electronic printer can type about 3,000 times faster. How many words is this per minute? _____ ; per second? _____

3. Did you know that the largest and slowest machine in the world, the *Crawler,* is responsible for taking the space shuttle to its launching pad? It weighs 3,000 tons and is 130 feet long and 115 feet wide. It travels at a speed of 2 miles per hour. The moon is 239,000 miles from the earth. If the *Crawler* were to travel to the moon instead of the space shuttle, how many hours would it take to get to there? _____ how many days? _____

Multicultural Math Fun: Holidays Around the Year

Mary Somerville

(1780–1872)

Mary Somerville was born in a small village on the seacoast of Scotland. When she was young, girls were discouraged from studying too hard for fear they might go mad. Mary Somerville, however, loved to study and taught herself French, Latin, and Greek. She learned the mathematics necessary to study the stars and chart the constellations. And she taught herself algebra and geometry. The subjects that fascinated her most were the ones related to her love of nature.

Somerville received many honors. Because she was one of the few women of her time who worked in the field of mathematics, she became especially famous. In honor of her love of nature, let's examine the mathematics of our moon.

1. The moon is the closest neighbor to the earth. Its average distance from the earth is about 239,000 miles.

   If a train traveled at a constant speed of 100 miles per hour, how long would it take to reach the moon? _____

2. Surface gravity on the earth is equal to 1; on the moon it is 0.17. How much would you weigh on the moon? _____

3. *Apollo* astronauts brought back to earth about 850 pounds of moon rocks. Find the cost of the *Apollo* missions if it cost about $1,900,000 to bring back each ounce of moon rock. _____

4. The largest crater we can see on the moon is called Bailly. It covers an area of about 26,000 square miles. Use your geography book and find countries that could fit into Bailly. _____
   _____

5. On earth, an astronaut in a space suit weighs about 300 pounds. On the moon, the astronaut's weight would be only one sixth as much. How much would the astronaut weigh on the moon? _____

Logical Mystery 1

The Rodriguez, McCarthy, and Hester families live in three houses on the same side of the street.

1. The Rodriguez family lives next to the McCarthy family.

2. There are no children in the middle house.

3. The family on the right does not own a poodle.

4. Kitty thinks her Labrador retriever is the best dog a person can have.

5. Gabby Rodriguez and Kitty Hester are good friends and attend the same middle school.

6. The Labrador retriever and the poodle are not neighbors.

Directions: From these clues, figure out which family lives in each house and who owns which dog.

Rodriguez: _____

McCarthy: _____

Hester: _____

Logical Mystery 2

Once upon a time there were three bears:

Marvin was the largest bear,

Mabel was a medium-sized bear, and

Mickey was the littlest bear.

They had three pots of porridge:

A large pot,

A medium-sized pot, and

A little pot.

Marvin was holding the medium-sized pot,

Mabel was holding the littlest pot, and

Mickey was really struggling with the largest pot.

They wanted to pass the pots around so that each was holding the pot that matched his or her size. However, they had to follow these rules:

1. Only one pot can be passed at a time.

2. If a bear is holding two pots, he or she can pass only the larger of the two.

3. A pot may not be passed to a bear holding a larger pot.

Directions: Determine the smallest number of passes needed so the three bears can solve their problem. You may want to begin by making three columns like this:

Marvin	Mabel	Mickey
M	S	L

5

Multicultural Math Fun: Holidays Around the Year

A Matrix Mystery

Directions: Use the 3 × 3 matrix and the clues to figure out which woman has which profession.

	Doctor	Lawyer	Architect
Maria			
Julia			
Olga			

1. Julia hates the sight of blood.

2. Olga and the lawyer play softball on the same team; last week they played the architect's team.

3. When the architect got married, Maria was maid of honor.

Mexican Independence Day Feast

Teacher Page

Fiesta Dinner
Tacos Verde, Blanco, y Rojo   **Buñuelos**
Green, White, and Red Tacos   Fried Sugar Tortillas
Ensalada de Calabacita   **Chocolate Mexicano**
Zucchini Salad   Mexican Hot Chocolate

Areas of study

ratio, proportion, fractions, rounding

Concepts

Students will

- find the conversion ratio
- use this ratio to enlarge recipes
- round their answers to appropriate measures

Materials needed

Mexican Independence Day Feast recipe sheets for each student, calculators

Procedures

Explain to students that September 16 is a national holiday in Mexico; it is the Mexican Independence Day. The recipes in the lesson are authentic Mexican dishes that you can prepare with your students.

Each recipe, as presented, feeds eight people. The conversion ratio is a ratio of the *new yield* (how many people you want to feed) divided by the *old yield* (how many people the recipe was written for). By multiplying the amount of each ingredient by this decimal ratio, you convert the recipe to feed the number of people in the new yield.

For example, if there are 20 students in the class, the ratio is $\frac{20}{8} = 2.5$; everything in the recipe needs to be increased $2\frac{1}{2}$ times. This conversion requires the rounding off of some of the amounts. For example, it is not possible to have $2\frac{1}{2}$ eggs.

Assessment

1. Student performance on the recipe sheet
2. Journal question: Explain the type of rounding off you needed to do when you converted the recipes.

Extension

If a kitchen is available for your use, prepare the feast with your students and actually celebrate Mexican Independence Day.

Name _____

Date _____

Mexican Independence Day Feast (page 1)

The following dishes are for a Fiesta Dinner to celebrate Mexican Independence Day. The recipes have been developed to serve eight people. Your job is to convert each recipe so that it will make enough food to feed your entire class.

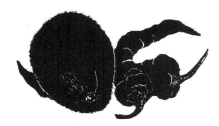

Tacos Verde, Blanco, y Rojo
1 small onion, chopped
1 tablespoon cooking oil
1 8-ounce can tomato sauce
$\frac{1}{2}$ teaspoon crushed red pepper
$\frac{1}{4}$ teaspoon salt
2 cups chopped cooked chicken
8 6-inch tortillas
2 cups guacamole
$\frac{1}{2}$ cup sour cream

Cook onion in oil until tender. Stir in next four ingredients. Spoon a little green guacamole, white sour cream, and red tomato/chicken mixture on each half of the tortillas.

Ensalada de Calabacita
4 cups sliced zucchini
1 cup white wine vinegar
$\frac{1}{4}$ cup oil
2 tablespoons sugar
1 clove garlic, minced
1 teaspoon basil
$\frac{1}{8}$ teaspoon pepper
lettuce
2 tomatoes, cut in thin wedges

Cook zucchini about three minutes in boiling water. Place zucchini in a $10 \times 6 \times 2$-inch dish. Combine next six ingredients and pour over zucchini. Cover and chill overnight. Serve over lettuce with tomatoes.

Buñuelos
$\frac{3}{4}$ cup milk
$\frac{1}{4}$ cup margarine
2 beaten eggs
3 cups flour
1 teaspoon baking powder
1 teaspoon salt
fat for frying

Heat milk and margarine to boiling. Cool. Stir in eggs. Sift together dry ingredients, add egg mixture, and mix. Shape into 16 balls (2 per person). Flatten and fry in deep hot fat until brown, turning once. Drain on paper towels. Sprinkle with powdered sugar.

Chocolate Mexicano
6 cups milk
$\frac{1}{2}$ cup sugar
3 squares chocolate (unsweetened)
1 teaspoon cinnamon
$\frac{1}{4}$ teaspoon salt
2 beaten eggs
2 teaspoons vanilla

In a saucepan, combine the first five ingredients. Heat, stirring, until the chocolate melts and milk is very hot. Gradually stir 1 cup of the hot mixture into the eggs; return to saucepan. Cook two minutes on very low heat. Add vanilla and beat until very frothy with a rotary beater.

Mexican Independence Day Feast (page 2)

Directions: Each of the previous recipes makes enough to feed eight people. If there were 30 people in your class, you would need to enlarge each recipe. To do this, you would need to set up the following fraction to find the conversion ratio:

$$\text{conversion ratio} = \frac{\text{new yield}}{\text{old yield}} \text{ or } \frac{30}{8} = 3.75$$

You would multiply each item in each recipe by 3.75. Do you have 30 people in your class? If not, how many are there? _____

Set up the conversion ratio formula and compute how much of each item you will need to make this Mexican Independence Day Feast for your class. Write the new amounts in the blanks provided in the recipes.

Tacos Verde, Blanco, y Rojo
____ small onion, chopped
____ tablespoon cooking oil
____ 8-oz can tomato sauce
____ teaspoon crushed red pepper
____ teaspoon salt
____ cups chopped cooked chicken
____ 6-inch tortillas
____ cups guacamole
____ cup sour cream

Cook onion in oil until tender. Stir in next four ingredients. Spoon a little green guacamole, white sour cream, and red tomato/chicken mixture on each half of the tortillas.

Ensalada de Calabacita
____ cups sliced zucchini
____ cup white wine vinegar
____ cup oil
____ tablespoons sugar
____ clove garlic, minced
____ teaspoon basil
____ teaspoon pepper
____ lettuce
____ tomatoes, cut in thin wedges

Cook zucchini about three minutes in boiling water. Place zucchini in a 10 × 6 × 2-inch dish. Combine next six ingredients and pour over zucchini. Cover and chill overnight. Serve over lettuce with tomatoes.

Buñuelos
____ cup milk
____ cup margarine
____ beaten eggs
____ cups flour
____ teaspoon baking powder
____ teaspoon salt
fat for frying

Heat milk and margarine to boiling. Cool. Stir in eggs. Sift together dry ingredients, add egg mixture, and mix. Shape into 16 balls (2 per person). Flatten and fry in deep hot fat until brown, turning once. Drain on paper towels. Sprinkle with powdered sugar.

Chocolate Mexicano
____ cups milk
____ cup sugar
____ squares chocolate (unsweetened)
____ teaspoon cinnamon
____ teaspoon salt
____ beaten eggs
____ teaspoons vanilla

In a saucepan, combine the first five ingredients. Heat, stirring, until the chocolate melts and milk is very hot. Gradually stir 1 cup of the hot mixture into the eggs; return to saucepan. Cook two minutes on very low heat. Add vanilla and beat until very frothy with a rotary beater.

What was the conversion ratio for your class? _____

The Legend of Bigfoot

Teacher Page

Areas of study

finding the area of irregularly shaped objects, approximation

Concepts

Students will

- approximate the area of their foot by finding the minimum and maximum areas
- approximate the area of their foot by gluing a traced outline on grid paper
- compare the two methods of finding the area of irregularly shaped objects

Materials needed

one-inch grid paper—two or three sheets per student, The Legend of Bigfoot instruction sheet for each student, glue and cellophane tape, scissors

Procedures

Discuss with students the legend of Bigfoot and how scientists were able to measure the size of a foot that is not a standard polygon. Ask students if they have any idea how big their foot is—not the shoe size, but the area of their foot.

There are two methods used to approximate the area of a foot.

Method 1: Students trace their foot on one-inch grid paper and find the minimum area (total number of squares inside the foot). Next they find the maximum area (total number of squares inside and on the boundary of the foot). The average of these two counts is a reasonable approximation.

Method 2: Students cut out around the outline of their foot and cut the footprint into squares. By tightly packing the squares on a second piece of grid paper and gluing them down, students can count the squares (see diagrams).

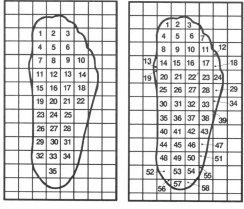

Method 1

Method 2

Assessment

1. Student products
2. Observation of students
3. Journal question: All of your answers are correct estimations of the area of your foot. Which do you think is best and why?

The Legend of Bigfoot (page 1)

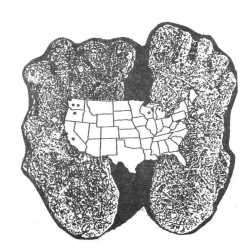

The Native Americans of the Pacific Northwest believed in a legendary Sasquatch, or Bigfoot. The Salish peoples of British Columbia tell legends of huge, strong-smelling, apelike creatures that lived in the deep woods. These legends have been passed on for hundreds of years. This creature supposedly had extremely large feet, measuring up to 18 inches long and 7 inches wide. But just how big is a big foot? How would you find the surface area of a big foot or your foot, which is an irregularly shaped object?

Directions

1. With the help of a partner, trace your left foot on one-inch grid paper. (*Now you know why your mother always wants you to wear clean socks.*)

2. Count the number of squares completely inside your traced foot. This is the minimum area of your foot. What is the minimum area of your foot?

   _____

3. Count the number of total squares inside your foot_____ and around the boundary or the edge _____ . Any part of a square counts as a full square. This is the maximum area of your foot. What is the maximum area of your foot? _____

4. The area of your foot is between the minimum and maximum area. The area of your foot is between _____ and _____ square inches.

5. One method of estimating the area of your foot is to find the average of the minimum and maximum areas. Calculate the average. What is the estimated area of your foot? _____

6. Cut out the outline of your foot. Carefully cut your foot outline into squares. Place these squares and pieces on another sheet of one-inch grid paper, and pack them as tightly as possible. Glue them on this second piece of grid paper. Count the number of squares covered by the pieces. This is another method to estimate the surface area of your foot. What is the estimated area of your foot using this method? _____
   How does it compare to the first estimated area you found by using minimum and maximum area? _____

The Legend of Bigfoot (page 2)
One-Inch Grid Paper

Indian Fry Bread

A delicious way to celebrate National Native American Day is by preparing Indian fry bread. It can be prepared in an electric skillet in your classroom.

Fry Bread	
5 cups flour 2 tablespoons baking powder 1 teaspoon salt 2 cups milk 1 tablespoon melted butter cooking oil	Sift flour with baking powder and salt. Combine milk and butter. Place flour in a large bowl and add liquid slowly. When all of the liquid has been added, knead to a smooth dough. Roll out $\frac{1}{8}$ inch thick. Cut with a biscuit cutter or glass. Fry in $\frac{1}{4}$ inch of oil. Fill with honey or jelly.

October Celebrations

Introduction

Have you ever played *Wheel of Fortune* and wondered about the frequency of each letter in the English language? By celebrating Noah Webster's Birthday (October 16, 1758), we honor the Father of the Dictionary while we search for an answer to this question.

The fall harvest is celebrated with Pumpkin Math, an activity that gives students hands-on experience with calculating the circumference of a sphere. And would October be October without the celebration of Halloween? An ancient celebration dating back to the sixth or seventh century, Halloween combines Druid autumn festivals with Christian traditions. In the spirit of a holiday associated with ghosts, goblins, and witches, students collect data with Count Chocula® cereal to find the percentage of different marshmallow creatures. Then they are asked to calculate the combination of Halloween costumes one can put together using three wigs, four shirts, and three pairs of pants. In the last problem, students contemplate the enormous numbers of legs they end up with when they start with just thirteen witches, each having seven sacks, each of which contains seven cats, etc.

Letter Frequencies

Teacher Page

Areas of study

estimation, mathematical predictions of future occurrences, data collection, organization, analysis, ratio/proportion/percent, averaging, communicating mathematically

Concepts

Students will

- collect data through a sampling activity
- organize the data to make predictions
- utilize information from a real-life activity
- explore frequency of occurrences in a variety of mathematical models

Materials needed

for each pair of students: one page of randomly selected reading materials, calculator, Letter Frequencies worksheets

Procedures

Before beginning the activity, ask pairs of students to predict which consonant they believe occurs the most frequently in the English language. Which vowel? Have them write their predictions on Letter Frequencies, page 1. Then give each pair of students a page of text material and ask them to count off 500 letters. They may start anywhere they wish, and the letters need not be in any special order. Tally marks may be used to count the frequency of each letter in their text. These marks should then be converted to frequencies, ratios, and percents. After pairs of students complete the data collection and computation activities, they complete the questions and journal entry. Conclude the activity by completing and discussing the Class Results sheet.

Assessment

1. Student performance on the data collection table
2. Observation of student pairs
3. Journal entry on the instructional sheet (page 1)

Extension

Have students develop a plan to estimate

- the average number of letters per line of text
- the average number of lines of text in the book
- the average number of letters in the book
- the probable frequency of each letter based upon the information obtained in this activity

Letter Frequencies (page 1)

What letters are most frequently used in written material in the English language? Get together with your partner and make a prediction. If you were to sample 500 randomly chosen letters, which consonant do you predict would appear the most often? _____ Which vowel?_____

Directions: Using a randomly chosen piece of reading material, count off 500 letters. Use the table (Letter Frequencies, page 2) to tally the number of times each letter appears. Record the frequency, the ratio, and the percent that each letter appears. After you complete the data collection, answer the following questions with your partner.

Questions

1. What percentage of your letters were consonants? _____

2. What percentage of your letters were vowels? _____

3. Is this what you expected to occur? _____

   Why or why not? _____

Journal

Write a paragraph describing how this information would help you if you were to appear on the TV program *Wheel of Fortune*. Be sure to include what you discovered about vowels and consonants. _____

_____

_____

_____

_____

_____

_____

_____

_____

_____

_____

_____

_____

Letter Frequencies (page 2)

Table

Letter	Tally	Number	Ratio	Percent
A				
B				
C				
D				
E				
F				
G				
H				
I				
J				
K				
L				
M				
N				
O				
P				
Q				
R				
S				
T				
U				
V				
W				
X				
Y				
Z				
TOTAL				

Letter Frequencies (page 3)

Class Results

GROUP	Percent of Vowels	Percent of Consonants	Ratio Vowels : Consonents
1			
2			
3			
4			
5			
6			
7			
8			
9			
10			
11			
12			
13			
14			
15			
MEAN			

What appears to be the ratio of vowels to consonants if we round our averages to the nearest whole number? _____

If we randomly count out 10 letters, how many vowels can we expect to have? _____ How many consonants? _____

Count out 10 letters with your partner three times. Does it work out that this is the probability of the occurrence of vowels to consonants?

Pumpkin Math

Teacher Page

Areas of study

estimation, measurement, data collection, circumference, percent of difference, and statistics

Concepts

Students will

- estimate the circumference of a sphere
- determine the percent of difference between their estimates and the actual circumference
- experience, in an intuitive way, the concept of deviation from the mean by working with absolute values of the difference

Materials needed

for each group of four: one small pumpkin, one skein of yarn or ball of string, one Pumpkin Math worksheet, one meterstick, calculators

Procedures

Each group member uses a length of yarn (or string) to estimate what he or she believes to be the distance around the group's pumpkin. After group members have made their estimates, they cut the yarn to the estimated length and measure it against the meterstick. Then group members take an *exact* measurement and cut a new piece of yarn to that length. This length of yarn is also measured against the meterstick and recorded as centimeters on the worksheet. The differences and percents of difference are computed for each member, and the means are found for the group. The group with the greatest percent of accuracy (smallest percent of difference) can be awarded a prize.

Assessment

1. Student performance in completing the table
2. Observation of student groups
3. Journal question: Did more of the students over- or underestimate the circumference? Why did this occur?

Extension

Have students estimate the number of seeds in their pumpkin. After they remove the seeds and decorate the pumpkin, have them count the seeds and do a percent-of-difference activity similar to the circumference activity.

Pumpkin Math

Directions

1. Each person in your group is to use yarn or string to estimate the distance around your pumpkin. Cut the yarn to the length you believe to be the circumference of your pumpkin. Measure it against the meterstick.
2. Now use a new piece of yarn to measure the actual distance around your pumpkin. Cut the piece of yarn at the exact length and measure it against the meterstick.
3. Record the data for your group on the table below and find the percent of difference for each member and the means.

	Estimate (centimeters)	Actual (centimeters)	Difference Absolute Value	Percent of Difference Difference/Actual
Member 1				
Member 2				
Member 3				
Member 4				
MEAN				

Which group members had the closest estimate?_____

the farthest away? _____

How many of your estimates were greater than the mean? _____

less than the mean? _____

Explain why you think this occurred. _____

_____

_____

Chocula Count

Teacher Page

Areas of study

data collection and analysis, estimation, ratio, percent, graphing, finding average

Concepts

Students will

- estimate the amount of cereal and marshmallows in their bag
- collect and analyze their data
- convert their sample data to ratios and percents
- graph the data in a circle graph
- find the average number of marshmallows in a box of cereal

Materials needed

for each pair of students: Chocula Count worksheets, two Pie Graph sheets, bag containing $\frac{1}{4}$ cup of Count Chocula cereal, protractors and rulers, calculators, markers/crayons/colored pencils for graph

Procedures

Before beginning the data collection, pairs of students should estimate the amount of cereal in their bag and write their estimate on the Chocula Count worksheet. A Sorting Sheet is provided for students to use when counting and sorting their cereal and marshmallow pieces. After counting and recording their numbers, students are to convert the data to ratios and percents. These numbers are used to design a circle graph of the data. Students can use proportion, for example,

$$\frac{\text{tan bats}}{\text{total pieces}} = \frac{n}{360°},$$ or percent, for example, $X\%$ of $360°$.

They then use a protractor to create a pie graph.

After groups have collected their data, they announce the number of marshmallows they had in their sample and record that number on the Class Results sheet. When an average is found, the average percent of marshmallow pieces in a sample and then in the entire box can be determined.

Assessment

1. Student performance on the data collection sheets
2. Accuracy of the circle graph
3. Observation of student groups
4. Journal questions:
   (a) Explain how you converted the number of tan bats to a percent of the total number of cereal pieces.

b. Explain the method you used to find the interior angles of your circle graph.
c. This box of cereal cost about $3.00. What percent of that did we pay for marshmallows? How many marshmallows is that? How much money did each marshmallow cost?

Extension

Have students explore the nutritional value of Chocula cereal and compare it with other cereals they like. They can also compare the price of this cereal with others to determine if it is a good buy.

Chocula Count (page 1)

Directions: Work with your partner to make five estimates: (1) how many total pieces of cereal you have in your bag, (2) how many tan bats are in the bag, (3) how many chocolate blobs, (4) how many brown howling wolves, and (5) how many yellow lightning bolts. Write your estimates in the space provided on the Estimate table below.

Now take an actual count of the cereal, *including the marshmallow pieces.* Then count how many of each type of marshmallow you have. Record this data on the Actual Count table below. Complete the table to find the ratio and percent of each of the marshmallows.

	Total Cereal Pieces Including Marshmallows	Tan Bats	Chocolate Blobs	Brown Howling Wolves	Yellow Lightning Bolts
ESTIMATE					

	Cereal Pieces Including Marshmallows	Tan Bats			Chocolate Blobs			Brown Howling Wolves			Yellow Lightning Bolts		
ACTUAL COUNT		#	Ratio	%	#	Ratio	%	#	Ratio	%	#	Ratio	%

The total number of marshmallow pieces in our sample was _____ .

How do you think this compared to the samples of other groups?

_____

_____

_____

_____

Chocula Count (page 2)

Sorting Sheet

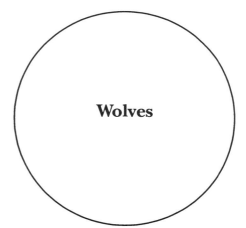

Bats

Blobs

Lightning Bolts

Wolves

Chocula Count (page 3)

Class Results

Group	Kinds of Cereal Pieces			
	Tan Bats	Chocolate Blobs	Brown Howling Wolves	Yellow Lightning Bolts
1				
2				
3				
4				
5				
6				
7				
8				
9				
10				
11				
12				
13				
14				
15				
AVERAGE				

Average number of marshmallow pieces: _____

Name _____

Date _____

Chocula Count (page 4)

Pie Graph

Directions: Graph the percentage in the circle below. Use the percent of each marshmallow to create a pie graph.

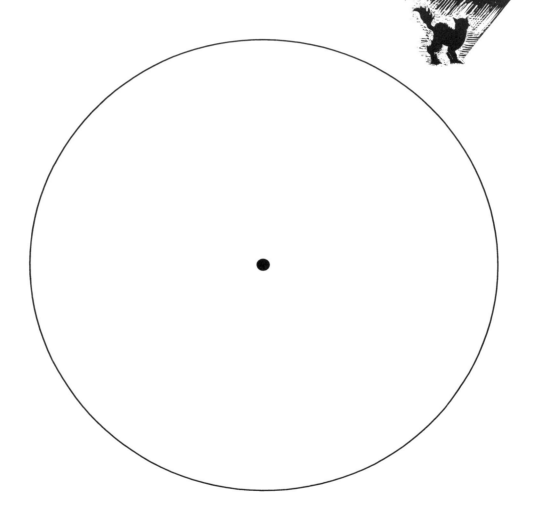

Title of Graph _____

Halloween Costumes

Samantha wants to be a clown for Halloween. She can choose a wig, top, and pants for her costume. How many different clown outfits can she make from the given items? _____

A Halloween Problem

There are thirteen witches. Each witch has seven sacks. In each sack there are seven cats. Each cat has seven kittens.

How many legs are there? _____

November Celebrations

Introduction

The first Tuesday after the first Monday in November is Election Day, but how many Americans vote? The first activity delineates the percentage of Americans who voted in the 1984 and 1988 presidential elections by states. Students will determine whether the percentages went up or down.

A few weeks later, on the fourth Thursday of November, Americans celebrate Thanksgiving. Legend tells us that the Pilgrims were saved from starvation with the help of the Native Americans. The Native American story "The Legend of How the Woodpecker Came to Be" tells us of the fate of a woman who refused to share her food with a hungry stranger. It is believed that folktales such as this might explain why the natives helped the early settlers.

The Thanksgiving Dinner project is a long-range project that allows students to design a menu, compile the necessary recipes, make a shopping list of foods needed to prepare the recipes, "shop" for the food, calculate the cost per person, and, finally, decide if they wish to eat at home or at a local restaurant. How do they make this decision? After researching the cost of dinner out, students can consider many options, including "best buy." Projects like these allow teachers to provide all students with substantive mathematics while acknowledging their different abilities.

Mark Twain's birthday is on November 30. What better way to recognize America's storyteller than by having our students read "The Celebrated Jumping Frog of Calaveras County" and by folding origami jumping frogs. Has anyone folded a champion frog? By having a jump-off, students collect and average data to find a class champion.

How Many Americans Vote?

Teacher Page

Areas of study

percent, ratio, reading tables, analyzing data, signed numbers, rounding

Concepts

Students will

- work collaboratively to find the percent of increase or decrease of Americans who voted in the 1984 and 1988 presidential elections
- analyze the data to determine which states had an increase and which states had the greatest decrease in voter turnout

Materials needed

calculators, How Many Americans Vote? worksheet for each student

Procedures

Discuss with students the formula for finding the percent of difference:

$$\text{percent of difference} = \frac{1988\,\% - 1984\,\%}{1984\,\%} \times 100$$

Discuss the outcome of positive results (an increase in voter turnout) and negative results (a decrease in voter turnout). In 1984, the two major candidates were Ronald Reagan and Walter Mondale; in 1988, the major candidates were George Bush and Michael Dukakis. Only three states had an increase in voter turnout in this election.

Students should round their answers to the nearest percent.

Assessment

1. Student products
2. Observation of students

Extension

Have students research and develop the data for the 1992 and 1996 presidential elections.

How Many Americans Vote?

Directions: The following table lists the percentage of Americans who voted in the 1984 and 1988 presidential election by states. Compute the percent of increase or decrease (round to the nearest percent). Then answer the questions following the table. An increase in voting should be indicated with a + sign; a decrease with a – sign. To find the percent of increase (+) or decrease (–), use this formula:

$$\text{percent of difference} = \frac{1988\,\% - 1984\,\%}{1984\,\%} \times 100$$

For example:

$$\text{Alabama} = \frac{46 - 50}{50} = \frac{-4}{50} = -.08 = -8\%; \text{ meaning 8\% fewer voted in 1988.}$$

State	1984 %	1988 %	% ±	State	1984 %	1988 %	% ±	State	1984 %	1988 %	% ±
Ala.	50	46	-8%	Ky.	51	48		N. Dak.	63	62	
Alaska	59	52		La.	55	51		Ohio	58	55	
Ariz.	45	45		Maine	65	62		Okla.	52	48	
Ark.	52	47		Md.	51	49		Oreg.	62	59	
Calif.	50	47		Mass.	58	58		Pa.	54	50	
Colo.	55	55		Mich.	58	54		R.I.	56	53	
Conn.	61	58		Minn.	68	66		S.C.	41	39	
Del.	55	51		Miss.	52	51		S. Dak.	63	61	
D.C.	43	39		Mo.	57	55		Tenn.	49	45	
Fla.	48	45		Mont.	65	62		Texas	47	44	
Ga.	42	39		Nebr.	56	57		Utah	62	60	
Hawaii	44	43		Nev.	41	45		Vt.	60	59	
Idaho	60	58		N.H.	53	55		Va.	51	48	
Ill.	57	53		N.J.	57	52		Wash.	58	55	
Ind.	57	53		N. Mex.	51	47		W. Va	52	47	
Iowa	62	60		N.Y.	51	48		Wis.	63	62	
Kans.	56	54		N.C.	47	43		Wyo.	53	50	

1. Only three states had an increase in voter turnout percentage. Which states were they? What were the increases? _____

_____

2. Which state(s) had the greatest decrease in their voter turnout percentage? What were the decreases? _____

Thanksgiving Dinner

Teacher Page

Areas of study

problem solving, computation, ratios/proportions, decimals, fractions, data collection

Concepts

Students will

- collect data over a period of time
- relate mathematics to a real-world problem
- convert recipes to serve a required number of people
- analyze and make decisions based upon data collected
- complete a project with multiple steps
- learn how to read and interpret newspaper advertisements

Materials needed

Thanksgiving Dinner instruction sheets for each student, local newspapers, recipes (either from home or from school), calculators

Procedures

Be sure to start this project at least two weeks prior to Thanksgiving. You might want to send a note to parents telling them: (1) what the project is and (2) how they might help their child obtain family recipes. Save newspapers with Thanksgiving advertisements for those students who might not have access to them.

Read through the project and discuss the various chapters with the students. Inform them that you will be grading the project in stages and give them the time limits they have to complete each chapter. The Teacher Checklist may be used as an assessment instrument.

Some students may not celebrate Thanksgiving in a traditional manner or serve traditional dishes. These students should be allowed to prepare a Celebration Dinner for a holiday of their choice.

Included in this unit is the Creek (Muskogee) legend "How the Woodpecker Came to Be," which tells the tale of a seemingly poor, hungry traveler who asks a woman for a little food. It is said that the Native American tradition of feeding hungry travelers is the foundation of the first Thanksgiving dinner.

Assessment

1. Student projects
2. Partial assessment based upon completion of each stage (see Teacher Checklist sheet that follows)
3. Overall quality of report

Extension

Have students prepare one of the dishes in their family meal for a class sampling. Copies of the recipes can be made available to place in a class Thanksgiving feast cookbook.

Thanksgiving Dinner

Teacher Checklist

Name of Student	Designing the Menu	Compiling the Recipes	Shopping List	Cost per Person	Restaurant	Home/ Restaurant

Thanksgiving Dinner (page 1)

Six-Part Project

1. Designing a Thanksgiving Day menu for your family

2. Finding the required recipes and adapting them for the number of people you need to feed

3. Compiling a shopping list of all of the items you need to purchase in order to make the dinner and determining the cost of these items

4. Computing the cost per person of the dinner based upon your shopping costs and the dinner you are making

5. Finding an advertisement for Thanksgiving dinner at a local restaurant

6. Determining if you choose to eat at home or out at the restaurant and why

This project is comprised of six "chapters" and must be designed and presented in a report folder. If possible, use a computer for your typing as well as your graphics.

Chapter 1: Designing the Menu

Discuss with someone in your family a typical menu for a Thanksgiving dinner. The menu should include an appetizer, a main dish, vegetables, side dishes, dessert, and beverages. Once you have outlined what you will serve, design a menu. Make it as attractive as you can, like a menu in a restaurant.

Chapter 2: Compiling the Recipes

Put together the recipes you need to complete your menu plans. Design one card for each of the recipes. Be sure to convert the recipes to allow for the number of people who will be at your dinner. For example, your recipe may call for $\frac{1}{2}$ cup of sugar to feed four people. If you have six people coming to dinner, you will need to use $\frac{3}{4}$ cup of sugar. Arrange the recipe cards attractively for presentation in the report folder.

Thanksgiving Dinner (page 2)

Chapter 3: Your Shopping List

Analyze your recipes and make a list of all the items you need to purchase to cook the meal. You will not need to purchase items if less than $\frac{1}{4}$ cup is needed and if the item would be commonly found in a home. An example might be 1 teaspoon salt.

Once you have made up your shopping list, you are ready to go to the supermarket and find the cost of the items (in the amounts you need) for your dinner. Write the cost next to each item on the list.

Chapter 4: Cost per Person

When you total your shopping list costs, you will know the total cost of the dinner. Now you need to find the cost per person.

Chapter 5: Researching a Restaurant

The fifth part of the assignment requires a little bit of research. You need to hunt through the local newspapers (we have some available if you do not have any at home). Find an advertisement for Thanksgiving dinner at a restaurant and neatly cut it out and include it in your report. Find the cost of feeding your family at this restaurant. You can now compare the cost of feeding your family at home to the cost of feeding your family at the restaurant.

Chapter 6: Eat at Home or at the Restaurant?

Carefully write two or three paragraphs that explain whether you think you would prefer to eat out or in, what you based your decision on, and how you feel others might make their decisions. Include any information that you feel is necessary to support the decision you made.

The Legend of How the Woodpecker Came to Be

A Story of the Muskogee People

Once upon a time there lived an old woman. Each day she wore a black dress, a white apron, and a red scarf tied around her head. The old woman was known throughout the land for her talent in making bread.

One day an old man came to her house. He was wearing an old coat and was tired and hungry. He said to the old woman, "I have walked many miles and am very tired. May I rest awhile before continuing on my journey?" He also asked, "Do you have some bread and water for this tired and hungry old man?"

The old woman said, "Yes, you may sit for awhile. I will go in and bake some bread so that you can have something to eat."

Then she went in the house, started the fire for the oven, and began to bake the bread. She noticed that she was running low on flour, but she knew she would have enough to make a pan of biscuits. As soon as the oven was hot, she put the biscuits in a pan and placed them in the oven.

The biscuits were soon done. When she took them out, she exclaimed, "These are the most beautiful, perfectly shaped biscuits I have ever made. These are too perfect to give to the old man." And so she kept them for herself.

She fixed another pan, but these were even more exquisite than the first. She decided to keep this batch for herself, as well.

She placed a third batch in the oven. When she removed these she exclaimed, "These are the most beautiful of them all. I can't give any of these to such a dirty old man!" She said, "Why should I give food to strangers, anyway?"

She went outside and told the old man that she had no bread to share with him. The old man knew that she was not telling the truth because he was really the Master of Life and he had been testing her.

He threw off his rags and said, "Something bad is going to happen to you because you would not share your bread." He stomped on the ground with his foot and the woman began to shrink until she was the size of a bird.

Her arms turned into wings . . . her black dress turned into black feathers . . . the white apron turned into white feathers . . . and the red scarf turned into red feathers on her head.

Master of Life said to the old woman, "Because you lied to me, from this day forward, you and all your descendants will have to peck wood to get your food."

Therefore, the elders of the Muskogee tribe say: It is good to share your food with strangers, even though you may have very little.

The Jumping Frog

Teacher Page

Areas of study

geometry, data collection, metric measurement, conversion within the metric system, averaging, listening to and following directions, connections with literature

Concepts

Students will

- listen to and follow directions in order to fold an origami frog
- use multiple trials to find the average distance their frog jumped
- measure and record their distances on the Class Record sheet
- find the record distance one of their frogs could jump
- make connections between mathematics and literature

Materials needed

for each pair of students: two sheets of $8\frac{1}{2} \times 11$ paper, scissors, Jumping Frog sheets

Procedures

You may wish to start the activity by reading excerpts from Mark Twain's "The Celebrated Jumping Frog of Calaveras County." Then give students the Origami Frog Folding sheet and have them follow oral directions for folding the frog. Students should be encouraged to fold with a partner so they can help each other through each step.

When the folding is complete, each student will have his or her frog jump three times and find the average distance jumped to the nearest millimeter. (The frogs jump because the paper unfolds.)

Determine a winner from each class and set up a time for each of the winning frogs to compete in a grade-level competition. Record these results on The Jumping Frog Class Winners sheet.

Assessment

1. Observation of student work
2. Journal questions:
    (a) Describe all the geometric shapes you can see in your jumping frog.
    (b) How many different types of triangles can you see in the frog? Sketch each of them as you describe them in your journal.
    (c) How many triangles can you find in step 5 on the Origami Frog Folding Sheet? (Perhaps a table would help.)

Extension

Have students research other origami animals, learn to fold them, and then teach the rest of the class how to make them.

The Jumping Frog (page 1)

Origami Frog Folding Sheet

1   Cut $8\frac{1}{2} \times 11$ paper in half lengthwise

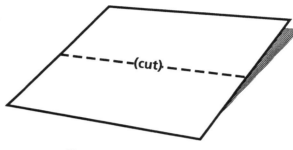

2   Fold this piece in half again

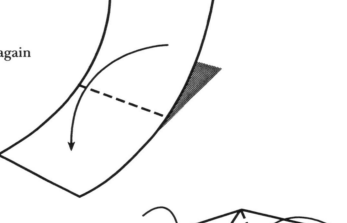

3   Fold corners down forming squares, trim excess

trim excess

4   Fold on diagonals as shown

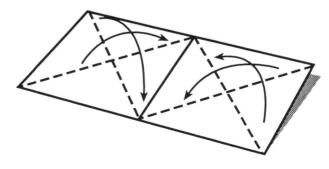

The Jumping Frog (page 2)

Origami Frog Folding Sheet

5 Now fold through the center of each square (solid lines are previous folds, dashed lines are current folds)

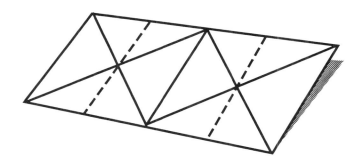

6 Fold left and right sides in compressing to form one square

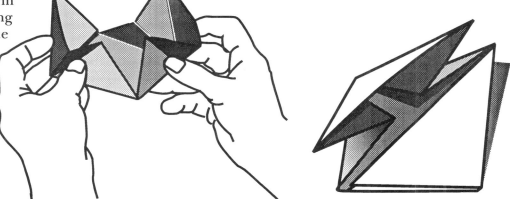

7 Fold four right triangles back to form legs

The Jumping Frog (page 3)

Origami Frog Folding Sheet

8 Fold over "paper airplane style" to complete legs

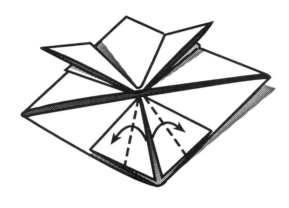

10 Fold up tail section, tuck in left and right flaps as shown

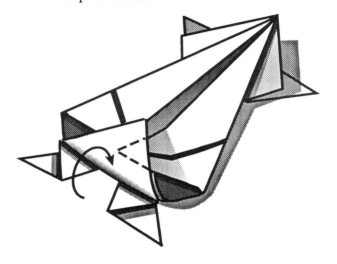

9 With legs down, fold to center as shown

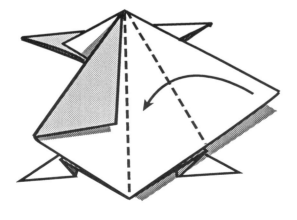

11 Form jumping frog by first folding under at A and back at B to create Z fold. Press at C to make jump.

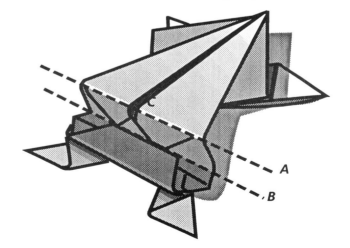

The Jumping Frog (page 4)

Class Record

Directions: Hold the folded frog on a flat surface and let go. As the paper unfolds, the frog should jump forward. Have it jump three times. Record your trials on the table below. Find the average. Use the average jump to see how you placed within the class.

Contestant's Name	Trial 1 (distance in centimeters)	Trial 2 (distance in centimeters)	Trial 3 (distance in centimeters)	Average (rounded to the nearest millimeter)

The Jumping Frog (page 5)

Class Winners

Now it is time for the winners in each class to compete for the grade-level championship. You will each take five trial jumps, and the average distance will be used to determine the winner. Line up at the starting line . . . .

Contestant's Class	Trial 1 (centimeters)	Trial 2 (centimeters)	Trial 3 (centimeters)	Trial 4 (centimeters)	Trial 5 (centimeters)	Average (rounded to the nearest millimeter)

December Celebrations

Introduction

Did you know that each snowflake is a unique hexagon? Celebrate the beginning of winter by using Japanese paper folding to make snowflakes. Students begin with an $8\frac{1}{2} \times 11$ sheet of paper, carefully follow directions to fold a hexagon, and then use their creativity to make their own unique snowflake.

Hanukkah: A Winter Holiday contains a make-your-own dreidel activity, the rules for playing the dreidel game, and some mathematical follow-up questions about the game. For added fun, you can ask students to try spinning a dreidel upside down (the dreidel that is, not yourself!).

The Winter Holidays shopping project tests the students' ability to spend. Students are told that they have won $1,000 from radio station WBIG just in time for the holiday season and are to use the money to buy gifts for their family and friends. At their mall, there's a 5% sales tax that they must add to the cost of the gifts. Their job is to spend as close to $1,000 (without going over) as they can. Can they spend exactly $1,000? If there are computers available to you, the shopping spree can be placed on a spreadsheet to improve the technology skills of your students. A sample spreadsheet has been included.

Three problems in Holiday Gifts add some intrigue to our holiday celebration. Do we use logic or algebra? These open-ended problems can be solved in many different ways. Encourage your students to explore their options and share their problem-solving strategies with the class.

Japanese Paper Folding: Snowflakes

Teacher Page

Areas of study

geometry, spatial visualization, connections

Concepts

Students will

- follow directions to fold a hexagon
- design a snowflake by visualizing the outcome of cuts
- make connections between art and math
- find linear and rotational symmetry in a snowflake

Materials needed

for each student: one sheet of $8\frac{1}{2} \times 11$ paper, scissors, Japanese Paper Folding: Snowflakes instruction sheet

Procedures

Follow the procedures as outlined on the instruction sheet. While students are folding their snowflakes, you may wish to ask them questions regarding:

- the area of each new shape
- size of angles
- the name of the shape
- lines of symmetry

When students have completed the folding and cut off the excess (step 6), have them open the shape to discover the hexagon. If they folded and trimmed carefully, this will be a regular hexagon. To make a snowflake, students need to refold the hexagon on the previous fold lines. By making decorative cuts in this shape, students can design their unique snowflakes.

Assessment

1. Observation of student products
2. Uniqueness of design

Japanese Paper Folding: Snowflakes

1 Fold a rectangular sheet of paper in half, as shown.

4 Fold vertex *A* so that it meets the fold line.

2 With the *closed* folded edge on top, fold in half again, as shown.

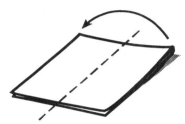

5 Fold a line from *B* to *D behind;* you are bisecting the angle at point *B*.

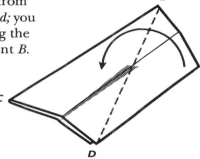

3 With the *closed* folded edge on the right, fold in half again, as shown, and open up

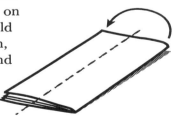

6 Cut through all layers at the point shown.

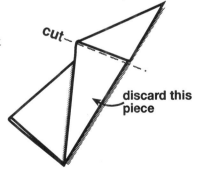

cut

discard this piece

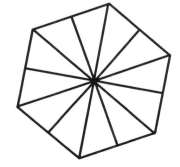

When unfolded, you have a hexagon. Refold and cut decoratively to form a snowflake.

Hanukkah: A Winter Holiday

Hanukkah, a holiday celebrated by the Jewish people around the world, celebrates the victory of Judah Maccabee over the Syrians in 165 B.C. The word Hanukkah means rededication and relates to the rededication of the Temple in Jerusalem. It is a joyous holiday celebrated with songs, games, and good food. One of the games played during this holiday is called dreidel. A pattern for the dreidel is provided on the Dreidel instruction sheet.

The dreidel is a four-sided top with Hebrew letters on each of the square sides. The four letters, nun, gimel, he, and shin mean "A great miracle happened here." Here are the rules to play this game of chance:

1. Each player needs about 20 tokens. These can be pennies or beans.

2. The players sit in a circle and a dish is placed in the center. This dish is called the pot. Each player must place 2 of their 20 tokens in the pot.

3. Players decide who goes first and then go, in turn, clockwise around the circle.

4. The first player spins the dreidel. When it stops, you must carefully observe which of the Hebrew letters is on top:
   nun—nothing happens, no tokens are taken out or placed in the pot, and the next player spins the dreidel.
   gimel—if this letter appears on top, the player takes all of the tokens in the pot. If a player spins a gimel, all players should add 2 tokens to the pot to keep the game going.
   he—the player takes half of the tokens from the pot.
   shin—the player must put 1 token into the pot.

5. The game continues until everyone has had at least 10 turns to spin the dreidel, or until everyone is tired. The person with the most tokens has won the game.

Probability is the likelihood that something will occur. For example, the probability that a "4" will occur on a roll of a die is 1 in 6.

What is the probability of any one of the letters appearing? _____

What is the probability that at the end of any spin a player will have more tokens than he or she started with? _____

Explain your answer. _____

What is the probability that you will end a spin with the same or fewer tokens than you started with? _____

Explain your answer. _____

Make Your Own Dreidel

Materials needed

one 15 cm × 20 cm piece of tagboard, scissors, glue or glue stick, small, thin wood skewer

Directions

1. Cut out the dreidel pattern along the solid lines and carefully trace it onto the tagboard.

2. Carefully fold along the dotted lines, using a ruler to help make the fold straight.

3. Glue the tabs inside the dreidel.

4. Carefully push the pointed end of the skewer through the center dot at the top of the dreidel and through the center of the triangles at the base.

5. You are now ready to play dreidel.

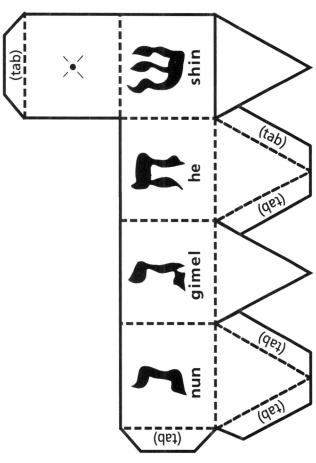

Holiday Shopping

Teacher Page

Areas of study
decimals, percentage, estimation, problem solving

Concepts
Students will

- research holiday catalogs or newspaper inserts to select gifts
- use mental math strategies to approach but not exceed $1,000
- compute costs and the amount of tax

Materials needed
catalogs and newspaper advertising inserts, Holiday Shopping worksheet for each student, calculators

Procedures
Collect mail-order catalogs and newspaper inserts ahead of time so that each of the students has a wide selection.

Begin the lesson by describing the worksheet and discussing the activity with your students. Talk about the need to choose appropriate gifts by thinking about the interests of the people for whom they are shopping.

Give the students enough time to view the catalogs and make their selections. If computers are available, and students need assistance with the formula, a sample spreadsheet for students to enter their purchases and compute the costs is as follows:

Holiday Shopping Spreadsheet

	A	B	C	D
1				
2	Holiday Project			
3				
4	Person	Cost	Tax	Total
5				
6			= B6*0.05	= B6 + C6
7			= B7*0.05	= B7 + C7
8			= B8*0.05	= B8 + C8
9			= B9*0.05	= B9 + C9
10			= B10*0.05	= B10 + C10
11				
12		Total		= Sum (D6..D10)
13				
14		Difference		= 1000 − D12

Assessment

1. Observation of student work
2. Journal questions:
   (a) List each of the people you purchased gifts for, tell what you bought, and give your reasons for purchasing these gifts.
   (b) Explain how 5% and 5¢ can be compared.
   (c) Explain how you might use "mental math" to find the tax.

Extension

- When ordering from a catalog, there are additional costs such as postage and handling. Ask students to add these costs to their purchase prices.
- If computers are available, ask students to design their own spreadsheet to do the computation.
- Substitute your community's tax rate for the 5%.
- Have students compute what percentage of their total costs each gift represents and what percent of the $1,000 they actually spent.

Holiday Shopping

Directions: Lucky you! You have won $1,000 from radio station WBIG just in time for the holiday season. You now have $1,000 to purchase holiday presents for five people.

1. List the five people for whom you will be buying presents.

2. List the purchases.

3. Complete the rest of the table.

You must come as close to $1,000 as possible—but you cannot spend any more! Be sure to add 5% tax to all of your purchases.

Person	Gift	Catalog	Cost	Tax (5%)	Total

Total cost of all of the gifts: _____

Amount not spent: _____

Name _____

Date _____

Holiday Gifts

1. John discovered a closet full of 22 holiday gifts. One of John's was the biggest and heaviest. His brother Sam had twice as many gifts as John. Noel has one more than twice as many gifts as Sam. Jill has two fewer than Noel. How many gifts will each child receive?

   _____
   _____
   _____

2. Santa wants to deliver your presents. How many different paths can he take to your house? He must stay on the streets—no shortcuts allowed.

   _____
   _____
   _____
   _____
   _____
   _____
   _____

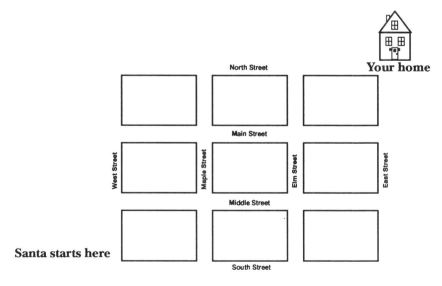

3. Lisa's parents purchased fewer than 100 holiday gifts. Lisa has one more gift than each of her siblings. She could have one, two, three, four, or five siblings and still have one more gift. How many gifts did her parents purchase?

   _____
   _____

Multicultural Math Fun: Holidays Around the Year

January Celebrations

Introduction

We start our January celebrations with an unusual day, Z-Day. This day, the very first day of the year, was contrived to recognize all those people and places whose names begin with the letter Z. These are the names that always appear last in any alphabetized list. After students solve the integer codes, they decode names of places and words that begin with the letter Z.

In January, we celebrate the birthday (January 15, 1929) of one of the most influential African-Americans to have lived in the twentieth century, Dr. Martin Luther King, Jr. In the I Have a Dream activity, Dr. King's famous speech is included, along with a map of the area in which the speech was presented. Students are asked to estimate the number of people who might have been present at this speech in 1963. This simulation develops estimation skills and shows students how experts assess the size of a crowd.

Z-Day

Teacher Page

Areas of study
integers, problem solving, decoding

Concepts
Students will
- use integers to decode words and countries
- use trial and error as a problem-solving strategy

Materials needed
Z-Day worksheet for each student

Procedures
Review the directions with the students to be sure that they understand the missing letter is different for each of the codes and the blank is their starting point. Once they choose the missing letter for the starting point, they move in a positive or negative direction from this letter to find the letter value represented by the integer.

Assessment
1. Student products
2. Observation of students

Extension
Have students create their own integer codes.

Z-Day

Z-Day is a very special holiday. It was invented to recognize people and places whose names begin with the letter Z. Does your name begin with the letter Z? Are you always listed last in an alphabetical list? What a treat to be recognized on the very first day of a new year!

Directions: The integers below represent letters in the alphabet. To decode the words you must

1. Find the missing letter.

2. Move the number and direction of spaces indicated by the integer from the missing letter. For example, if you think the missing letter is *m* and you have to move +3, then you move to the right and the missing letter would be *p*.

3. You cannot move beyond the end of the alphabet in either direction. So if you are told to move +14, the missing letter cannot be an *m* because this would take you beyond *z*.

   Here's an example.

   <u>+1</u> <u>–10</u> ___ <u>–6</u> <u>–16</u> <u>–24</u>   a type of grass

   missing letter = y
   word = zoysia

Use the alphabet here to help you make your moves.

a b c d e f g h i j k l m n o p q r s t u v w x y z

1. <u>+17</u> <u>–8</u> ___ <u>+9</u> <u>–4</u>   country in Africa

2. <u>+8</u> <u>–13</u> ___ <u>–3</u>   numerical symbol, nothing

3. <u>+23</u> <u>+6</u> <u>+9</u> ___ <u>+5</u>   blank, empty

4. <u>+13</u> <u>–12</u> ___ <u>–11</u> <u>–4</u> <u>–12</u>   another country in Africa

5. <u>+5</u> ___ <u>–7</u> <u>–12</u>   Indian tribe

                   Multicultural Math Fun: Holidays Around the Year

I Have a Dream

Teacher Page

Areas of study

measurement, area, data
collection, estimation

Concepts

Students will

• mark off a 3-square-foot area

• determine the density of population that is comfortable for this area

• compute, based upon their experiment, the number of people who watched
   Dr. Martin Luther King's speech

• analyze the accuracy of previous estimations

Materials needed

yardsticks, calculators, I Have a Dream worksheets for each group of students

Procedures

Students can work on this project in groups of six. Find an appropriate spot for
students to measure out a 3-square-foot area for their group. Students need to
stand in their spot with a reasonably comfortable density. The space will probably hold four to six students, depending on size and shape. Once the density is
established for a 9-square-foot area, students compute the possible density for
the area as outlined on the worksheet.

Assessment

1. Student products and analysis of density
2. Observation of students

I Have a Dream (page 1)

Dr. Martin Luther King, Jr. (1929–1968)

Dr. Martin Luther King, Jr., has been called the most influential African American to have lived in the twentieth century. In order to better understand the reason we celebrate his birthday, let's take a personal look at the man and the famous speech that he made in 1963. They are an important part of our history.

Because of his small stature, King was the target of school bullies. Always opposed to violence, he learned to talk his way out of trouble. He finished high school in only two years and entered Morehouse College at the age of 15.

He was inspired by the writings of Henry David Thoreau and Mahatma Gandhi. These writings directed him toward his future cause—the nonviolent crusade for civil rights.

At the age of 26, Dr. King was chosen president of the newly formed Southern Christian Leadership Conference. Through this organization he was instrumental in organizing the March on Washington, August 28, 1963. It is estimated that 250,000 people from across the United States met that day and heard what has come to be known as the "I Have a Dream" speech.

Dr. King received the Nobel Peace Prize in 1964. Four years later he was killed by an assassin's bullet in Memphis, Tennessee. How ironic that a man who so abhorred violence should have his life ended so violently. Following is the famous speech that he delivered at the Lincoln Memorial.

So I say to you, my friends, that even though we must face the difficulties of today and tomorrow, I still have a dream. It is a dream deeply rooted in the American dream that one day this nation will rise up and live out the true meaning of its creed—we hold these truths to be self-evident, that all men are created equal.

I have a dream that one day on the red hills of Georgia, sons of former slaves and sons of former slave-owners will be able to sit down together at the table of brotherhood.

I have a dream, that one day, even the state of Mississippi, a state sweltering in the heat of injustice, sweltering with the heat of oppression, will be transformed into an oasis of freedom and justice.

I have a dream my four little children will one day live in a nation where they will not be judged by the color of their skin but by the content of their character. I have a dream today!

I have a dream that one day, down in Alabama, with its vicious racists . . . little black boys and black girls will be able to join hands with little white boys and white girls as sisters and brothers. I have a dream today!

I Have a Dream (page 2)

I have a dream that one day every valley shall be exalted, every hill and mountain shall be made low, the rough places shall be made plain, and the crooked places shall be made straight and the glory of the Lord will be revealed and all flesh shall see it together. This is our hope. This is the faith that I go back to the South with.

With this faith we will be able to hew out of the mountain of despair a stone of hope. With this faith we will be able to transform the jangling discords of our nation into a beautiful symphony of brotherhood.

With this faith we will be able to work together, to pray together, to struggle together, to go to jail together, to stand up for freedom together, knowing that we will be free one day. This will be the day when all of God's children will be able to sing with new meaning – "my country 'tis of thee; sweet land of liberty; of thee I sing; land where my fathers died, land of the pilgrim's pride, from every mountainside, let freedom ring"—and if America is to be a great nation, this must become true.

So let freedom ring from the prodigious hilltops of New Hampshire.

Let freedom ring from the mighty mountains of New York.

Let freedom ring from the heightening Alleghenies of Pennsylvania.

Let freedom ring from the snowcapped Rockies of Colorado.

Let freedom ring from the curvaceous slopes of California.

But not only that.

Let freedom ring from Stone Mountain of Georgia.

Let freedom ring from Lookout Mountain of Tennessee.

Let freedom ring from every hill and molehill of Mississippi, from every mountainside, let freedom ring.

And when we allow freedom to ring, when we let it ring from every village and hamlet, from every state and city, we will be able to speed up that day when all of God's children—black men and white men, Jews and Gentiles, Catholics and Protestants—will be able to join hands and sing in the words of the old Negro spiritual, "free at last, free at last, thank God Almighty, we are free at last."

I Have a Dream (page 3)

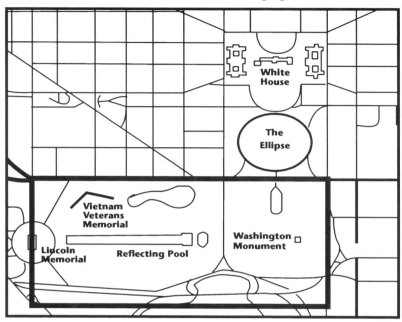

The map above shows the area where Dr. Martin Luther King, Jr., gave his famous speech in 1963. The total dimensions of the rectangle are 1,500 feet by 5,000 feet. However, in aerial photographs it appears that people were only standing in an area that was 900 feet by 4,000 feet. It has been estimated that about 250,000 people were in this area listening to the speech. Just how crowded would people be as they stood at this historic event?

Directions:

1. Mark off a 3 × 3-foot area.

2. Join with as many classmates as you can to fill the area comfortably. Be sure you would be comfortable standing and listening to speeches for a few hours.

3. How many students can comfortably stand in this area? _____

4. What is the area of the space occupied by the crowd in 1963? _____

   _____

5. Compute, based upon your experiment, how many people could have comfortably listened to Dr. King. _____

Do you believe the estimate of people watching Dr. King's "I Have a Dream" speech was reasonable? Explain your answer. _____

_____

_____

February Celebrations

Introduction

February is another exciting month for celebrations. We begin by watching for a furry rodent who determines whether we will have six more weeks of winter. If the groundhog sees his shadow, he scurries back into his burrow and we wait for spring. In honor of Groundhog Day, Our Shadow Knows has students use ratio and proportion to determine the height of objects.

February is also celebrated as Black History Month. We have three activities to commemorate the heritage and contributions of African Americans. The first, Kenya's Birthday Celebration, emphasizes the importance of birthdays in Kenyan culture. Why remember Kenya during our February celebration? Although very poor, the people of Kenya believe that birthdays should be celebrated. We look at their birthday celebrations though a data collection activity. The accomplishments of George Washington Carver are highlighted in two data collection activities, How Many Peanuts Can You Hold? and How Many Peanuts in a Pound? While examining the achievements of a great African American, students estimate, measure, work with percents, and explore statistics with real-life data.

And what holiday does everybody love? Valentine's Day, of course! Another data collection activity, Valentine Vowels, has students counting the number of vowels on candy hearts and then displaying their collection on a circle graph.

Finally, the third Monday in February, Presidents' Day, is celebrated with a probability experiment, Presidential Toss. Based on the area of a grid, students compare actual and theoretical probability.

Our Shadow Knows

Teacher Page

Areas of study

ratio and proportion, measurement, data collection and analysis, computation

Concepts

Students will

- collect data through measurement
- work collaboratively in groups
- record and analyze data
- calculate the mean
- draw conclusions and make predictions on data collected

Materials needed

Our Shadow Knows worksheet for each group of students, linear measuring tools (sticks or tapes), calculators, trees, and a sunny day

Procedures

After placing students in groups of four or five, discuss how ratio and proportion can be used to solve problems in which three of the variables are known and the fourth is unknown. Then have students problem solve which of the elements of the proportion can be measured easily.

The heights of students can be measured more easily before going outside to measure shadows.

Assessment

1. Student products on worksheets
2. Observation of student groups
3. Journal questions:
   (a) Develop a problem that could be solved more easily by using ratio and proportion.
   (b) Why did we find the mean height and mean shadow length for use in our proportion?
   (c) In the morning or afternoon, your shadow will be longer than at noon. Will this make a difference in (1) your calculations or (2) the height of the tree?

Extension

Have students investigate sundials as a timekeeping mechanism.

Our Shadow Knows

Directions: Complete the following steps in groups of five:

1. Measure the height of each member. Record that measurement on the table below.

2. Measure the length of each member's shadow. Record that measurement on the table below.

3. Measure the length of the shadow of a tree. Record that measurement below the table.

4. Find the
   (a) mean individual height
   (b) mean individual shadow length

   Record the means on the table.

Member	Member's Height	Length of Member's Shadow
1		
2		
3		
4		
5		
MEAN		

Tree's shadow length: _____

You can use this ratio to help you find the height of the tree:

$$\frac{\text{tree's shadow length}}{\text{group mean shadow length}} = \frac{\text{tree's height}}{\text{group mean height}}$$

We find that our tree is _____ tall.

Kenya's Birthday Celebration

Teacher Page

Areas of study

data collection and analysis, stem-and-leaf plots, graphing

Concepts

Students will

- create a bar graph with the dates of their births
- change the data to a stem-and-leaf plot

Materials needed

one set of months per class, birthday card for each student, scissors, markers

Procedures

Give each student a birthday card and have him or her fill in the blanks.

For example, if a student were born on February 8, he or she would write a large 8 on the birthday card and then sign his or her name in the indicated spot.

Cut apart the months and paste them on the chalkboard (or mount them on a bulletin board) with enough space below for students to place their cards (see the example).

Jan	Feb	Mar	Apr	May	June	July	Aug	Sept	Oct	Nov	Dec
Mary	Luis	Joey	Ann	Jane	Scott	Amy	Alice	Julia	Jean	Bob	Cal
Juan	Tobi			Pete	Keisha	Tom			Beth		Bill
Teri				Dave							
				May							
				Josh							

This display will be a concrete bar graph for the students.

From this collected data, have students design a stem-and-leaf plot:

```
1 | 2  3  5  7     The numbers in the stem represent the month of their birth.
2 | 1  8
3 | 7          2 | 1    stands for February 1.
```

Assessment

1. Student products
2. Observation of students

Kenya's Birthday Celebration

Cut apart on dotted lines. Prepare one copy of birthday card for each student.

_____ Day of the Month of Your Birthday _____ Your Name	_____ Day of the Month of Your Birthday _____ Your Name
_____ Day of the Month of Your Birthday _____ Your Name	_____ Day of the Month of Your Birthday _____ Your Name
_____ Day of the Month of Your Birthday _____ Your Name	_____ Day of the Month of Your Birthday _____ Your Name

Kenya's Birthday Celebration

January	**February**
March	**April**
May	**June**

Kenya's Birthday Celebration

July	**August**
September	**October**
November	**December**

65

How Many Peanuts Can You Hold?

Teacher Page

Areas of study

data collection, statistics, measurement, scatterplot graphing, stem-and-leaf plots

Concepts

Students will

- measure to the nearest millimeter
- collect personal data
- compare their data on a scatterplot and look for positive correlation
- organize their data on a stem-and-leaf plot
- find the range, mean, median, and mode of their data

Materials needed

overhead transparencies of the three How Many Peanuts Can You Hold? sheets, copies of the three sheets for each student, about two pounds of unshelled peanuts, calculators, metric rulers or metersticks

Procedures

Make an overhead transparency of the Class Record sheet. Have each student measure the span of his or her hand and then grab a handful of the unshelled peanuts. Tell the students to be careful that the peanuts have not extended beyond the boundaries of their hands. Have students write their (a) name, (b) hand span, and (c) the number of peanuts they held on the Class Record sheet. Each student should have the data for the whole class. If you wish, students can find the averages for the class.

Once the data have been collected, use the Stem-and-Leaf Plot to organize it in a meaningful way. This is an example of a completed plot:

```
0 |
1 | 2   3   5   7     The numbers in the stem represent the tens digit.
2 | 1   8
3 | 0                     2 | 1    stands for 21 peanuts.
```

Give each student a copy of the Stem-and-Leaf Plot sheet. Use an overhead transparency for them to follow.

Once students have completed this graph, they are ready to record the data about their hand span and number of peanuts on the Scatterplot. There should be a positive correlation; as the hand span increases, so should the number of peanuts a student can hold.

Assessment

1. Observation of students
2. Journal questions:
   (a) Explain why there is considered to be a positive correlation between the size of your hand span and the number of peanuts you could hold.
   (b) Which measure of central tendency (mean, median, or mode) do you think best helps you analyze the data? Why?

Extension

Have students create other scatterplots that have a positive correlation or a negative correlation.

How Many Peanuts Can You Hold? (page 1)
Class Record

Directions: We are going to take two different measurements to conduct this mathematical experiment. First, measure the span of your hand to the nearest millimeter. Then grab a handful of unshelled peanuts and count how many you have in your hand. You **cannot** have peanuts extending beyond the boundaries of your hand. Record your data on the following chart.

Name of Student	Hand Span (in millimeters)	Number of Peanuts in Hand

How Many Peanuts Can You Hold? (page 2)

Stem-and-Leaf Plot

Use this "stem" to help you analyze the data your class collected. How many peanuts could most of the students hold?

0
1
2
3
4
5
6
7
8
9

What was the range of peanuts that students in this class could hold? _____

Find the median._____ Is there a mode? _____ If yes, what is it? _____

Find the mean number of peanuts each student could hold. _____

How Many Peanuts Can You Hold? (page 3)

Scatterplot

Record the results of your hand span and number of peanuts here.

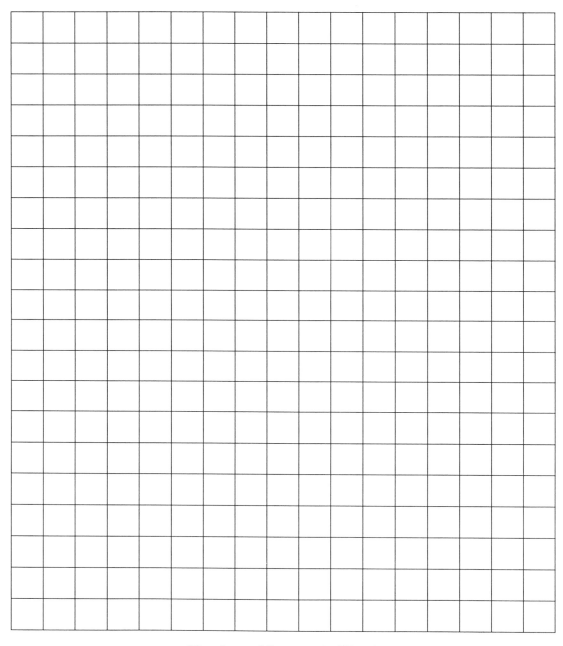

Hand Span (in millimeters)

Number of Peanuts in Hand

Multicultural Math Fun: Holidays Around the Year

How Many Peanuts in a Pound?

Teacher Page

Areas of study

data collection, estimation, computation, percent, measurement, averaging

Concepts

Students will

- collect data by accurately weighing peanuts
- make predictions about the weight of the data
- compute the percent of error
- compute the percent of peanut that is edible
- compute the cost of the edible part

Materials needed

for each group: unshelled peanuts, a scale, calculator, How Many Peanuts in a Pound? worksheets; overhead transparency of Class Results sheet

Procedures

Discuss the worksheet with the class. Place students in groups of four and give each group the materials they need to complete the experiment. Stress the need for careful measurements. Explain that a class average will be obtained to help with accuracy. To determine the cost of the edible parts of the peanut, use the following proportion:

$$\frac{\text{cost per pound of peanuts (\$1)}}{\text{weight of shelled peanuts (in oz)}} = \frac{x}{16\,\text{oz}}$$

After all of the groups have completed the experiment, enter their data on the Class Results sheet and find the average for the class.

Assessment

1. Quality of data collection sheets
2. Observation of students
3. Journal questions:
   (a) Explain the procedures you used to compute the percent of error.
   (b) Explain the procedures you used to compute the cost of the edible part.
   (c) For what other foods are we charged for both the edible and the inedible parts? Name as many as you can.

Extension

Have students conduct similar experiments with bananas, oranges, other types of nuts, etc.

How Many Peanuts in a Pound?

Directions: In your group, complete the following steps and answer the questions:

1. How many unshelled peanuts do you think it would take to weigh a pound? Make a prediction and write it here:

   _____

   Now, working in your groups, place unshelled peanuts on a scale until you have one pound. Try to be as accurate as you can.

   How many peanuts are there in a pound? _____

   How far off was your estimate? _____

   What is your percent of error? _____

$$\text{percent of error} = \frac{\text{amount of error}}{\text{total weight}}$$

2. How much do you think this pound of unshelled peanuts would weigh if you shelled them? Write your prediction here: _____

   Now shell your peanuts and weigh them again.

   How much do they weigh? _____

   What percent is this of the original weight? _____

$$\text{percent} = \frac{\text{weight without the shell}}{\text{weight with shells}}$$

3. If the peanuts cost $1 per pound unshelled, how much are we paying for the edible part? *Hint:* Set up a proportion where one of the ratios is the cost ($1) of the edible weight.

   In the following space, explain how you solved this problem.

   _____

   _____

   _____

   _____

   _____

   _____

How Many Peanuts in a Pound?

Class Results

Group	Number of Unshelled Peanuts per Pound	Weight of Unshelled Peanuts	Ratio of $\frac{\text{Shelled}}{\text{Unshelled}}$	Percent of Edible Parts
1				
2				
3				
4				
5				
6				
7				
Average				

Valentine Vowels

Teacher Page

Areas of study

data collection, organization, analysis, fractions, percent, graphing, angle measurement, computation

Concepts

Students will

- collect data from valentine candies
- express data in fraction and percent form
- find the degrees in a circle their data represents
- graph the data in a circle graph

Materials needed

$\frac{1}{8}$ to $\frac{1}{4}$ cup of valentine candies with valentine messages in a plastic bag for each pair of students, Valentine Vowels frequency table and circle graph for each pair of students, calculators, markers/crayons/colored pencils, protractors, rulers

Procedures

Before beginning the activity, have students predict which vowel they think will appear most in their collection. Give each pair of students a bag of candy and allow them time to complete their data collection, analysis, and graphing.

Assessment

1. Student products
2. Observation of students
3. Accuracy of circle graph
4. Journal question:
    (a) Were you surprised by the results of your data collection? Why?
    (b) How did your data compare to the data of other groups?

Valentine Vowels (page 1)

Directions: In this activity, you will determine which vowel or vowels appear most frequently on valentine candies. After collecting your data, you will analyze and graph it. Use the valentine candies in your bag to complete the frequency table below. Before you begin, predict the vowel(s) you think will appear most often in your collection. Write your prediction here:

_____

_____

Vowel	Frequency	Fraction	Percent	Degrees in a Circle
A				
E				
I				
O				
U				
Totals				

 Multicultural Math Fun: Holidays Around the Year

Valentine Vowels (page 2)

Directions: Graph your results on the circle provided below. Use the percent of each vowel to find the degrees it represents of the 360° circle.

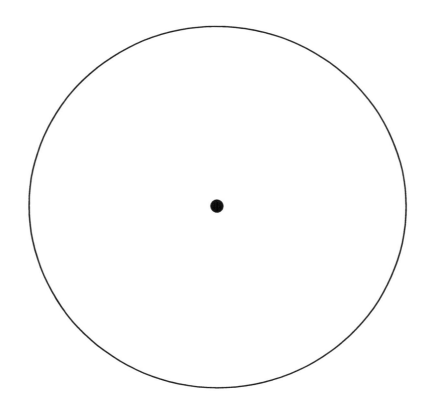

Title of the graph: _____

Presidential Toss

Teacher Page

Areas of study

experimental and theoretical probability, data collection and analysis, ratio and proportion, area, radius, diameter, averages, mathematical connections to social studies

Concepts

Students will

- collect data from coins tossed on the grid
- calculate the experimental probability based upon data collected
- find the class average probabilities
- determine radius and diameter of each coin to compute theoretical probabilities

Materials needed

penny, nickel, dime, and quarter for each group of students, Presidential Toss sheets for each group, calculators, metric rulers with millimeter measurements

Procedures

This activity allows students to experiment with different-sized coins and determine whether their size will affect their placement on the grid. Discuss with students what is meant by tossing a coin on the grid and what a fair coin toss is. What will be considered a hit, a miss, or out of play? Experimental probability is the ratio of hits to total tosses.

Place students in groups of two to four and distribute tally sheets, grids, and coins. After individual groups have completed their data collection, place the results on the Class Data sheet and find class averages.

The Theoretical Probability sheet may be used as an extension activity to allow students the opportunity to compare their experimental and theoretical probabilities. Students measure the diameter and calculate the radius of each coin, and record their data. The theoretical probability of a coin landing inside the square is the ratio of the *winning area* to the *total area*. The winning area is determined by subtracting the radius of the coin from each side of a grid square. The diagram shown reflects the measurements of a penny: the diameter of a penny is 20 millimeters, so 44 millimeters (the size of each edge on the grid) minus 20 millimeters (the size of the square formed by the penny's diameter) equals 24 millimeters (the side of each edge of the winning area).

Assessment

1. Students' products on worksheets
2. Observation of student groups
3. Journal questions:
   (a) Discuss how the size of the coin affects the probability of a win.
   (b) How did your data compare to the class average?
   (c) How does the theoretical probability compare to the experimental probability? What could cause the differences (discuss this for each coin)?

Name _____

Date _____

Presidential Toss (page 1)

Coins on a Grid

Presidential Toss (page 2)

Data Collection

Which president is the luckiest?

Directions: Toss each coin on the square grid 100 times. If the coin lands entirely within the square, the toss is a win or a **hit**. If the coin lands on or touches a line, it is a loss and is tallied as a **miss**. Record your data on the chart below. Calculate each probability.

To calculate the experimental probability, find the ratio of hits to total tosses. Your ratio will look like this:

$$\text{experimental probability} = \frac{\text{hits}}{\text{total tosses}}$$

Coin	President	Tally of Hits	Tally of Misses	Total	Experimental Probability
Penny					
Nickel					
Dime					
Quarter					

Multicultural Math Fun: Holidays Around the Year

Name _____

Date _____

Presidential Toss (page 3)
Class Data Sheet

Record the experimental probability for each group on the table below. Find the class average probability.

Experimental Probability

Groups	Penny	Nickel	Dime	Quarter
1				
2				
3				
4				
5				
6				
7				
8				
9				
10				
11				
12				
13				
14				
Average				

Presidential Toss (page 4)

Theoretical Probability

How could we calculate the theoretical probability, using the size of each coin?

Directions: Measure the diameter (in millimeters) of each coin, calculate the radius (half the diameter), and record the data on the table below.

To calculate the theoretical probability, find the ratio of winning area to total area of the square (see diagram below). Your ratio will look like this:

$$\text{theoretical probability} = \frac{\text{winning area}}{\text{total area}}$$

Coin	President	Diameter of Coin (in millimeters)	Radius of Coin (in millimeters)	Theoretical Probability
Penny				
Nickel				
Dime				
Quarter				

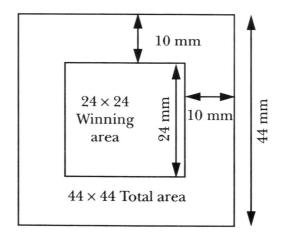

Measurements not to scale

Multicultural Math Fun: Holidays Around the Year

March Celebrations

Introduction

March celebrations begin on March 3 with a data collection activity honoring the birthday (1847) of the Scottish-born inventor Alexander Graham Bell. Students will discover how telephone numbers are distributed—a real-world application of random numbers.

Did you know that March 14 is Pi Day (no, π is not misspelled). Pi Day is celebrated on 3/14 or 3.14! To commemorate this remarkable ratio, we have a few circular activities. The first is the Pizza Survey. What are the students' favorite toppings on pizza? What do you like best? The next, Pennies and π, is a probability simulation that approximates the value of π. And finally, in Amazing π, students discover the remarkable relationship between the circumference and diameter of a circle.

The final celebration for the month of March is the wearing of the green. Two activities, Lucky Charms® and Shamrocks and Bunnies, help us celebrate St. Patrick's Day—the day we all "become Irish." Tell students to bring their appetite when they do the Lucky Charms activity because they must *dispose* of the data properly. Be sure to allow students to share their reasoning after they have discovered how many shamrock leaves the bunnies have eaten and how many remain.

Telephone Tally

Teacher Page

Areas of study
random numbers, prediction of trends, variation from the mean, frequency charts

Concepts
Students will

- organize data in a frequency table
- explore the concept of random numbers
- evaluate data to predict future trends
- be introduced to the concept of variation from the mean
- learn how to deal with messy data

Materials needed
strip of a minimum of 50 telephone numbers per student, Telephone Tally worksheets for each student

Procedures
Give students a strip of telephone numbers and ask them to predict which number they believe will appear most often. They must record their results before they begin to collect their data. Have them count down 50 telephone numbers and draw a line under the fiftieth number. Each student tallies the last four digits of each number and records the frequency, ratio, and percent for each of the digits 0 through 9. Since there are 200 digits, equivalent fractions can be set up and percent can be found intuitively by dividing their ratio in half. Have each student record his or her results on the Class Record sheet. Determine an average for the class.

After all of your classes have completed the experiment, record the class averages on the Grade-Level Results sheet. In this way, you can find an average for the entire grade level.

Pull the lesson together with questions such as:

- Do you see a trend?
- Do you still believe that one digit appears more often in the formation of telephone numbers?
- Why do you think we took a class average? A grade-level average?

Assessment
1. Student performance on activity sheets
2. Observation of students
3. Journal questions:
   (a) What does randomness mean?
   (b) Do you believe the digits in telephone numbers are chosen randomly? Why or why not?

Extension
Have students use supermarket ads from the newspaper to tally the digits as they appear in 25 ads. Are the results the same? different? Why?

Telephone Tally (page 1)

If you were to count off the last four digits of 50 telephone numbers, which number do you think would occur most often? Record your prediction here:

_____

Let's see if your prediction is correct!

Directions: Count down 50 numbers and draw a line under the fiftieth telephone number. Use tally marks (卌) to record only the last four digits of each number on the table below. Record the frequency, the ratio, and the percent of times each of the digits appears.

Digit	Tally	Frequency	Ratio	Percent
0				
1				
2				
3				
4				
5				
6				
7				
8				
9				
Total				

When you have completed your data collection, add your results to the Class Record sheet.

Telephone Tally (page 2)

Class Record

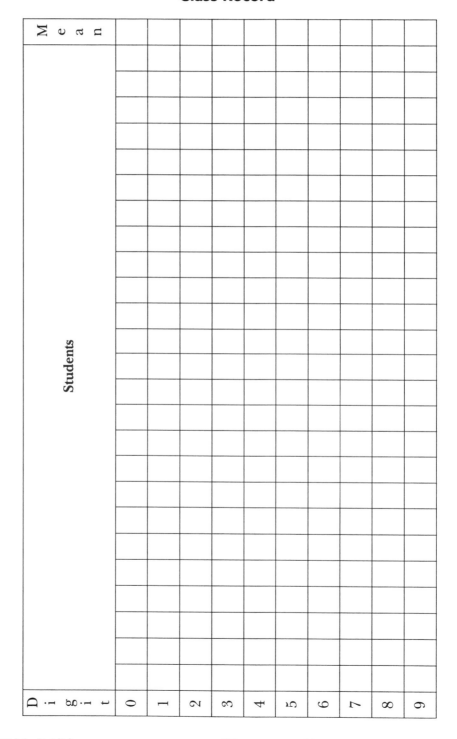

	Mean											
Students												
Digit	0	1	2	3	4	5	6	7	8	9		

Telephone Tally (page 3)

Grade-Level Results

Record the frequency with which each digit appears in each class.

Digit	Class #1	Class #2	Class #3	Class #4	Class #5	Class #6	Mean
0							
1							
2							
3							
4							
5							
6							
7							
8							
9							

Does one digit appear more often than others?
What percent of the time does each digit seem
to occur?

Pizza Survey

Teacher Page

Areas of study

data collection, fractions, decimals, percents, graphing, computation

Concepts

Students will

- collect, organize, analyze, and interpret data
- convert frequencies to fractions, decimals, and percents
- determine the number of degrees in the interior angles for pizza-preference pie graph
- construct a pie graph to present their data
- compute the cost of each type of pizza and determine least and most expensive

Materials needed

Data Collection Chart, Circle Graph, and Pizza Menu sheet for each student or pair of students, calculators, crayons/markers/colored pencils, protractors, rulers

Procedures

Introduce this Pi Day activity by asking students which pizza they believe will be the most popular of the choices given on the Data Collection Chart sheet. Then have students, working alone or with a partner, survey 30 people to find which is the most popular. They tally their results, converting to a frequency, fraction, decimal, and percent, and finally to the number of degrees necessary to correspond to the interior angles of a pie (π) graph. They can use the percent of 360° or set up a ratio and use proportions to find the number of degrees.

The next step is for students to design a pie graph to represent their data. Encourage them to be creative, perhaps by having each section resemble the type of pizza it represents in the survey.

Finally, have students use the menu to compute the cost of a large pizza with each of the ingredients listed to determine the least and most expensive.

Assessment

1. Successful completion of data collection sheet
2. Observation of students
3. Journal questions:
   (a) Describe the steps you used to convert your tally to a frequency, to a fraction, a decimal, a percent, and finally to the degrees needed for the pie shape in your pie graph.
   (b) What other type of graph could you have used to describe this data? Why?

Extension

Have students develop their own survey question and design a data collection table. After they conduct the survey, have students draw a graph and write a short report describing what they discovered.

Pizza Survey (page 1)
Data Collection Chart

Directions: Use the data collection chart below to record the pizza preferences of 30 people. Tally their responses and then complete the rest of the chart. Design a pie graph to interpret the results you obtained.

Predict what type of pizza will be the most popular. Write your prediction here: _____

Type of Pizza	Tally	Frequency	Fraction	Decimal	Percent	Degrees of a Circle	Cost of a Large Pizza
Cheese							
1/2 Sausage							
Pepperoni							
Green Pepper & Onion							
1/2 Mushroom & 1/2 Sausage							
Total							

Was your prediction correct? _____ Look at the menu provided with this survey to find the cost of each type of pizza. Which would be the most expensive? _____ The least expensive? _____ Why? _____

Pizza Survey (page 2)

Circle Graph

Directions: Use the circle below to design a pie graph to display the results of your pizza survey.

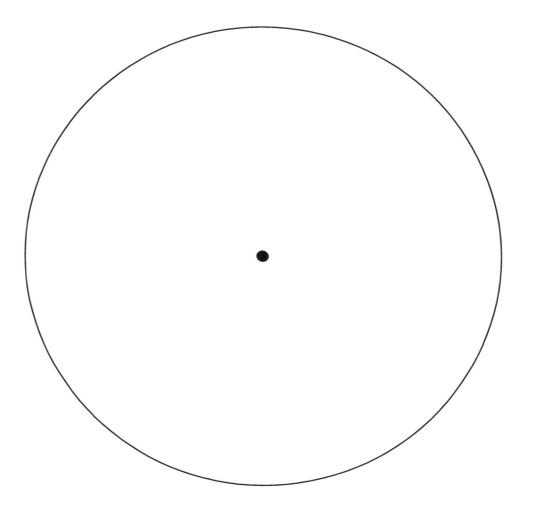

Title of your graph: _____

Pizza Survey (page 3)

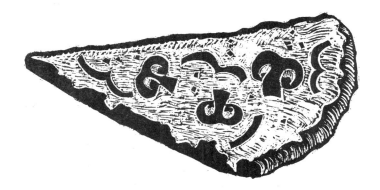

Build Your Own Pizza on a Cheese Base

	10" small	12" medium	14" large	16" x-large
All Cheese	$5.95	$6.95	$7.95	$9.95
New York Style—Double-Thick Dough	.75	1.00	1.25	1.50
Pan, Deep-dish	1.50	1.75	2.00	2.25
Stuffed	1.75	2.00	2.25	2.50
Each Extra Ingredient on Half	1.00	1.25	1.50	1.75
Each Extra Ingredient All Over	1.25	1.50	1.75	2.00

Pennies and π

Teacher Page

Areas of study

data collection, substitution for a variable, statistics

Concepts

Students will

- collect data to establish a relationship
- substitute for variables in an equation
- approximate the value of π through experimentation
- understand that multiple trials can be used to improve the validity of data

Materials needed

for each student pair: one penny, Pennies and π sheets

Procedures

Have students work in pairs to record the number of hits and misses (as defined on the Data Collection sheet) they have in 100 tosses of a penny. The formula $\frac{4h}{t}$ can be used with other coins as long as a new grid is made. The distance between the centers of the dots must be equal to the diameter of the new coin.

After individual pairs record their results and their ratio of hits to tosses, record the results on the Class Data sheet. Work with students to determine a class ratio.

Assessment

1. Computation on data collection table
2. Observation of students
3. Journal questions:
   (a) Describe the procedures you and your partner used to find the approximation of π ratio. Why did we combine the data of all of the groups into one class data ratio?
   (b) What do you think would happen to the value of π if we used a different coin, such as a dime or a quarter?

Pennies and π (page 1)

Data Collection

Pi (π) is a fascinating number. We use it all the time to help us find the circumference and area of circles. We can use this experiment to help us approximate the value of π.

Directions: Toss a penny 100 times so that it lands on the dot board. Count only the tosses that land completely inside the border. When a penny touches or covers a point, tally a "hit"; when it doesn't touch a point, tally a "miss."

Hit	
Miss	

After you toss the penny 100 times, use this formula to estimate the value of π: *t = times* and *h = hits.*

$$\frac{4h}{t} = \text{_____}$$

How close to π is your number? _____

Pi (π) is approximately

3.141592658979323846264338327950288419716939937510582097494459230781 . . .

Pennies and π (page 2)

Data Collection Grid

Pennies and π (page 3)

Class Data

Directions: Use the table below to enter your data. We will add your data to that from other teams to increase our number of trials.

Teams	Number of Hits	Number of Tosses
Total		

Find the class ratio of hits to tosses using $\frac{4h}{t}$: _____

Amazing π

Teacher Page

Areas of study

circumference, diameter, rounding, data collection, averaging, measurement, ratios

Concepts

Students will

- measure to the nearest millimeter
- develop an understanding of circumference, diameter, and the ratio π
- round decimals
- convert fractions to decimals
- find the mean for a set of data

Materials needed

Amazing π worksheet for each pair or group of students, cylinders (cans) of at least 10 different sizes, metric tape measures, calculators

Procedures

Place students into groups of two or three. Give each group of students a copy of the worksheet, a metric tape measure, and a calculator. Instruct groups to carefully measure the circumference and diameter of each cylinder. After groups have completed the measurements, discuss the following questions:

- What is the relationship between the circumference of a circle and the diameter?
- Is it what you thought it might be?
- If you wanted to walk around a perfectly circular lake that was 30 miles in circumference, what would the distance be if you could walk through the middle? Other questions may evolve from the discussion but the major point of emphasis should be the constant of pi(π).

Assessment

1. Student products
2. Observation of students
3. Journal questions:
   (a) If you knew the circumference of a circle and the value of π, how would you find the diameter?
   (b) Why didn't everyone calculate the same value for π?
   (c) Why do we celebrate Pi Day on March 14?

Amazing π

How does the circumference of any circle compare with its diameter? Make a prediction. _____

Directions: Measure the circumference of each of 10 different cylinders, using your metric tape measure. Record the measurement to the nearest millimeter. Now measure the diameter (be sure to measure as carefully as you can). Record your measurement to the nearest millimeter. Set up the ratio as indicated on the table below. Use your calculator to convert the ratio to its decimal equivalent. Express your answer to the nearest hundredth. When you complete the measurements, find the mean ratio (expressed as a decimal).

Cylinder	Circumference	Diameter	Ratio c/d	Decimal

The mean decimal ratio is _____

Lucky Charms®

Teacher Page

Areas of study

estimation, data collection, ratio, percent, percent of difference, pie graphs

Concepts

Students will

- estimate the number of marshmallows in their sample
- understand the fraction or ratio of each to the total number
- find the percent each of the marshmallows represents in their sample
- find the percent of difference between their estimate and their actual count
- analyze and compare their results with the class results
- compute the size of each pie-shaped region for their graph
- graph their data in a pie graph

Materials needed

for each student pair: sandwich bag containing $\frac{1}{4}$ cup of Lucky Charms, Lucky Charms sheets, calculator, compasses, rulers, markers/crayons/colored pencils

Procedures

Have students work in pairs. Give each pair a sandwich bag containing $\frac{1}{4}$ cup of cereal. The student pairs predict and record the number of marshmallows they think are in their bag.

Using the Data Collection sheet, students sort the marshmallows, count each type, and record their results. Using these results, they complete the rest of the table, finding the ratio, percents, and degrees needed to graph each of the sections of the pie graph. Students may use calculators to compute their answers.

Pairs of students then prepare a pie graph of the results of their data collection. When they have completed their graphs, they record their results on the Class Results sheet. Class averages can be determined when all of the pairs have entered their data.

Assessment

1. Computation on the Data Collection table
2. Observation of students
3. Journal questions:
   (a) Describe how you converted the ratio of marshmallow to a percent. Give an example.
   (b) Describe how you computed the number of degrees in each angle of your pie graph. Give an example.
   (c) How did your results compare with the class average? Why do you think this occurred?

Extension

Have students count all of the cereal pieces and marshmallows in their bag. Then have them compute the ratio of marshmallows to the total (cereal and marshmallows) to determine the percentage of marshmallow in the box of cereal.

Lucky Charms (page 1)

Data Collection

You have been given $\frac{1}{4}$ cup of Lucky Charms cereal, which contains cereal pieces and marshmallow bits. Predict how many pieces of marshmallow you have in your bag. Write your prediction here:

_____

Directions: Sort and count the actual number of marshmallows. Use the Sorting Sheet to spread out your cereal for easier counting. Record your count and complete the table below.

Marshmallow Piece	**Frequency**	**Ratio** $\dfrac{\text{Individual}}{\text{Total}}$	**Percent of Marshmallow**	**Degrees of Circle**
Purple Horseshoe				
Blue Moon				
Green Clover				
Orange Star				
Pot o'Gold				
Pink Heart				
Red Balloon				
Rainbow				
Total				

What was the total number of marshmallows in your sample? _____

How far away from the actual number was your estimate? _____

What is your percent of difference? (this is a ratio of difference to the total)

_____

$$\text{percent of difference} = \frac{\text{difference}}{\text{total number of marshmallows}} \times 100$$

Lucky Charms (page 2)

Class Results

Group	Purple Horseshoe	Blue Moon	Green Clover	Orange Star	Pot o'Gold	Pink Heart	Red Balloon	Rainbow	Total
1									
2									
3									
4									
5									
6									
7									
8									
9									
10									
11									
12									
13									
14									
15									
Average									

Lucky Charms (page 3)

Sorting Sheet

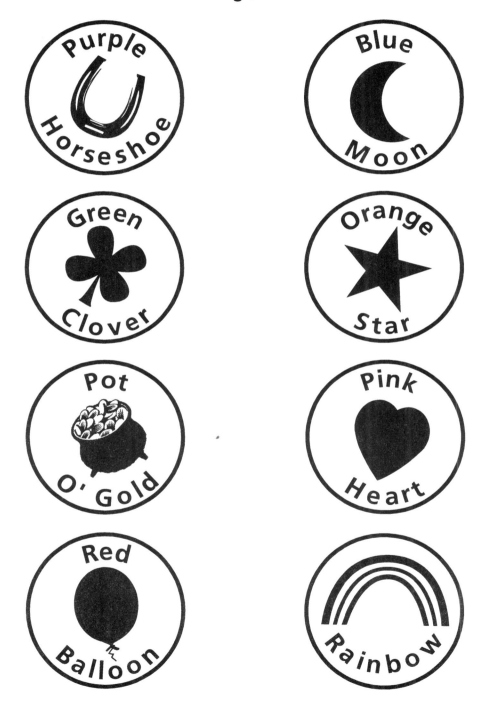

Lucky Charms (page 4)

Graph

Directions: Create a pie graph to show the percentages of the different types of marshmallows.

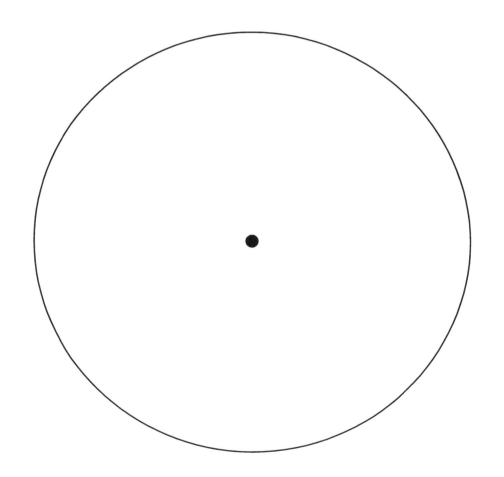

Our graph's name: _____

Shamrocks and Bunnies

A family of bunnies found seven shamrocks growing by an old elm tree. The littlest bunny ate five shamrock leaves. The mama bunny ate three shamrock leaves, and the papa bunny left one leaf on three shamrocks. How many of the shamrock leaves were left growing? _____

April Celebrations

Introduction

It's April Fool's Day and we all know what that means! If you're asked a question, be sure to listen very carefully! For example, you have two coins worth 30¢ and one of them is not a nickel. How can this be? Well, . . . *

And although March is the beginning of spring, the season really gets under way in April. So, what better way to celebrate spring than by eating jelly beans? But we can't just eat them. Remember, this is a math class. Students will estimate the number of jelly beans in the bag, collect and analyze data, find the percent of each color, and create graphic representations of their data. They probably thought the only thing jelly beans were good for was eating!

---

* Answer: The other one is! Get it?

April Fool's Mathematics Test

Directions: Answer each question carefully. Remember today is April Fool's Day!

1. If an individual went to bed at 8 o'clock in the evening and set the alarm to get up at 9 o'clock in the morning, how many hours sleep would he or she get? _____

2. Do they have a Fourth of July in England? _____

3. How many birthdays does the average person have? _____

4. Can a person living in Chicago, Illinois, be buried west of the Mississippi River? _____

5. If you had a match and entered a room in which there was a kerosene lamp, an oil heater, and a wood-burning stove, which item would you light first? _____

6. Some months have 30 days, some 31; how many have 28? _____

7. If your doctor gave you three pills and said, "Take one every half hour," how long would they last? _____

8. How far can a dog run into a forest? _____

9. Divide 30 by $\frac{1}{2}$ and add 10. What is your answer? _____

10. How much dirt can be removed from a hole that is 4 feet deep, 2 feet wide, and 5 feet long? _____

Jelly Bean Count

Teacher Page

Areas of study

data collection, estimation, ratio, percent, angle measurement, bar graphs, circle graphs

Concepts

Students will

- collect and record data in an experimental setting
- set up ratios
- calculate percent and angle measurements
- construct both a bar and a circle graph

Materials needed

for each pair of students: sandwich bag of 20 jelly beans (can be purchased in the bulk food sections of the supermarket), Data Collection and Graphs sheets, markers or colored pencils, protractors and rulers, calculators (if needed)

Procedures

Give each pair of students a sandwich bag of jelly beans. Have them estimate the number of jelly beans in their bag and record this estimate. Student pairs then count and record the number of each color on their sheets. Have students set up ratios ($n/20$). These can be converted to percents by setting up the proportion. Student pairs then graph their results in both bar and circle formats.

Assessment

1. Student products
2. Observation of students
3. Journal questions:
   (a) Would it be unusual to find 12 white jelly beans in a bag of 20? Is it possible?
   (b) Using your data, about how many white jelly beans would you expect to find in a bag of 200 jelly beans?

Name _____

Date _____

Jelly Bean Count (page 1)

Data Collection

How many jelly beans do you estimate there are in the bag you have been given? Write your estimate here: _____

Directions: Count the number of each color of jelly bean and record the number on the table below. Then complete the remaining columns of the table. Record the ratio of color to total.

Color	Frequency	Ratio	Percent	Degree of a Circle
Red				
Yellow				
Pink				
White				
Green				
Purple				
Black				
Orange				
Total				

Jelly Bean Count (page 2)

Graphs

Directions: Draw a circle graph of your jelly bean data in the circle below. Be sure to color in the sections and label the percent of each color.

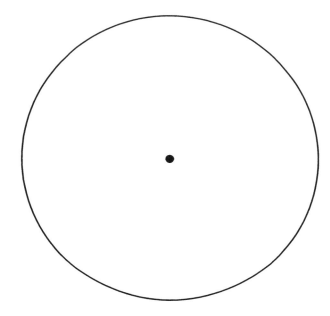

Now create a bar graph of your results.

May Celebrations

Introduction

Another busy month of celebrations! The month begins with Cinco de Mayo, the Mexican national holiday recognizing the anniversary of the Battle of Puebla (1862). The Mexican troops, led by General Ignacio Zaragoza and outnumbered three to one, defeated the invading French armies of Napoleon III. In Mexico the holiday is celebrated with parades and speeches. In our mathematics class, we will celebrate with 5/5—Using Five 5's and Population of Mexico's Cities. The first activity is a very interesting puzzle: Students form the numbers 1 through 10 using five 5's. The second will give students an understanding of how many people live in the cities in Mexico.

During the first week of the fifth month of the year, the people of Japan celebrate Children's Day, and we celebrate in our mathematics classroom with Million Grains of Rice. How big a container would you need to hold 1,000,000 grains of rice? Could you use a soda can, a large bowl, a big bucket, or a truck? An interesting problem for the students in your class.

May 14 (1686) is the birthday of Gabriel Fahrenheit, a German physicist. He developed a scale for measuring temperature with the freezing point of water at 32° and the boiling point of water at 212°. Two activities help us celebrate Fahrenheit's birthday. The first, Temperature Highs and Lows, asks students to convert Celsius temperatures to Fahrenheit. The second, The Highest and Coldest Mountains, asks students to compute how cold it would be at the top of a mountain if it were room temperature at the base.

Students flying paper airplanes in mathematics class? Well, this is exactly what you ask them to do to celebrate Charles Lindbergh's birthday on May 20. Lucky Lindy, a data collection activity, uses multiple trials and averages to help students find the champion class pilot.

5/5
Using Five 5's

Mexico

Directions: Use five 5's, and any of the operations of arithmetic, to form the numbers 1 through 10.

Example:

$$(5-5) \times 5 + \tfrac{5}{5} = 1$$

Population of Mexico's Cities

Teacher Page

Areas of study

percent, problem solving, reading a chart, numeration

Concepts

Students will

• find the percent of Mexico's population living in each major city

• use ratio and proportion to solve problems

Materials needed

Population of Mexico's Cities worksheet for each student, calculators

Procedures

Show students how to use proportions to solve the problems. Be sure students understand the process. Have students set up proportion for each city as follows:

$$\frac{x\%}{100} = \frac{\text{city's population}}{88,335,000} \times 100$$

For example, to find the percent of population for Mexico City:

$$\frac{x\%}{100} = \frac{20,207,000}{88,335,000} \approx 0.23 \times 100 = 23\%$$

Answers should be rounded to the nearest tenth of a percent. Students should find total percent of population since it should approximate 100.

Assessment

1. Student products

2. Observation of students

3. Journal question: The total population of Mexico is 88,335,000 and the area is 761,604 square miles. On average, how many people are there per square mile?

Population of Mexico's Cities

Directions: Use the information on the table to find the percentage of Mexico's population living in each of Mexico's major cities.

The 1990 population estimate for Mexico was 88,335,000 people.*

Major Cities	Population	Percent of Population
Mexico City	20,207,000	
Guadalajara	3,262,000	
Monterrey	2,837,000	
Puebla	836,000	
León	656,000	
Ciudad Juarez	567,000	
Culiacán	560,000	
Mexicali	511,000	
Tijuana	461,000	
Mérida	425,000	
Acapulco	409,000	
Chihuahua	407,000	
San Luis Potosí	407,000	
Hermosillo	341,000	
Mazatlán	250,000	

* Data obtained from *The World Almanac and Book of Facts,* 1992, and *PC Globe*

Million Grains of Rice

Teacher Page

Areas of study

measurement, estimation, data collection, statistics, equivalent units, sampling

Concepts

Students will

- determine the number of grains of rice in a small measure and calculate an estimate for a much larger amount
- find the mean, median, range, and mode of the data
- convert from tablespoons to cups to quarts to gallons
- determine the appropriate size container to hold 1,000,000 grains of rice

Materials needed

one tablespoon for each pair, calculators, one paper plate per pair to place rice on, one pound of rice per class, Million Grains of Rice data collection sheet for each pair of students

Procedures

Have students form pairs and give each pair one measured tablespoon of rice. Student pairs then count the exact number of grains of rice in their sample and report their findings to the class. Pairs record the class data on their own worksheet, arranging the data from least to greatest. These data are used to calculate the range, mean, median, and mode.

Using the class mean, students now know the average number of grains of rice in a tablespoon. The next step is to compute the number of tablespoons in 1,000,000 grains. This is not an appropriate measure to use for such a large quantity; the equivalency table can be used to convert tablespoons to a more appropriate measure. Students can now problem solve to find a suitable container for 1,000,000 grains of rice.

Assessment

1. Successful completion of data sheet
2. Observation of students
3. Journal question: How would you determine the appropriate container to hold 1,000,000 pieces of popped popcorn?

Extension

The average American consumes $16\frac{1}{2}$ pounds or $34\frac{1}{4}$ cups of rice per year (weight and measure is for uncooked rice). Have students compute the approximate number of grains of rice the average American eats per year.

Name _____

Date _____

Million Grains of Rice

Rice is a staple of the Japanese diet. Rice is also the major agricultural crop of Japan. What size container would you need to carry 1,000,000 grains of rice? Could you use a soda can, a large bowl, a wastepaper basket, a car trunk, a pickup truck bed, a semitrailer, a train car, or an entire train? Taking a sample will help you find out what size container will be needed to hold 1,000,000 rice grains.

Directions: With your partner, measure one tablespoon of rice onto a paper plate. Count the number of grains of rice in one tablespoon. Collect the data from all the pairs and calculate the range, mean, median, and mode.

Use the collected data to determine the:

Range_____   Mean _____

Median _____   Mode _____

Equivalent Measures
16 tablespoons = 1 cup
4 cups = 1 quart
4 quarts = 1 gallon

Divide 1,000,000 by the average number of rice grains in one tablespoon to find the number of tablespoons in 1,000,000 rice grains. Use the Equivalent Measures table to find:

Number of tablespoons _____

Number of cups _____

Number of quarts _____

Number of gallons _____

What size container would be best to carry 1,000,000 rice grains?

_____

Group	Grains in Tablespoon	Data Least to Greatest

Temperature Highs and Lows

All the earth's heat and light comes from the sun. The sun keeps the temperature of most of the earth's surface at between –50° C and +50° C. In the United States, we still record temperature using a scale named after a German physicist, Gabriel Fahrenheit. We can convert temperatures recorded on the Celsius scale to the Fahrenheit scale by using the following formula:

$$F° = (\frac{9}{5} \times C°) + 32$$

By using this formula we see that the sun keeps most of the earth's surface between –58° F and +122° F.

Directions: The temperatures listed below are record highs and lows. Use the formula above to convert these to the Fahrenheit scale.

Place	Temperature in ° Celsius	Temperature in ° Fahrenheit
Death Valley, California	57° C	
Tirat Tsvi, Israel	54° C	
Seville, Spain	50° C	
Vostok, Antarctica	–89° C	
Snag, Yukon	–63° C	
Ilfrane, Morocco	–24° C	

The Highest and Coldest Mountains

Did you know that the higher you go up a mountain the colder it becomes? Since air cools as it rises, the temperature drops 11° F for every 3,300 feet.

Directions: What if it were 68° F at the base of each of these mountains? What would the temperature be at the very top? Use the information above to find the correct temperature for each mountain.

Highest Mountain by Continent				
Continent	**Location**	**Name of Mountain**	**Height (in Feet)**	**Temperature at the Top**
North America	Alaska	Mount McKinley	20,320	
South America	Argentina	Mount Aconcagua	22,834	
Africa	Tanzania	Mount Kilimanjaro	19,340	
Asia	Nepal/Tibet	Mount Everest	29,028	
Eastern Europe	Russia	Mount Eibrus	18,510	
Western Europe	France	Mont Blanc	15,771	
Antarctica	Ellsworth Land	Vinson Massif	16,864	
Oceania	New Zealand	Mount Cook	12,349	

Lucky Lindy

Teacher Page

Areas of study

data collection, metric measurement, arithmetic mean, mathematical connections, collaborative learning

Concepts

Students will

- work collaboratively to gather data
- record and analyze their data
- find the arithmetic mean to find a *typical* incident
- compare their results with other teams

Material needed

paper airplane that students design, metersticks or measuring tape for each team (a trundle wheel works well), clipboard for each team, calculators, paper and cellophane tape, Lucky Lindy sheets for each team

Procedures

Students form teams of four, and each team member designs a paper airplane. To determine the best flyer for a team, each team member will take three trials and find the average distance flown. The trials can be conducted in long hallways or, preferably, outdoors. When the winner for each team has been determined, that airplane is flown 10 times and an average is taken. These distances are recorded on the Group Analysis sheet and a class winner is determined. Multiple trials are run and an average taken to disallow very long or very short flights. The average is a more accurate representation of the capabilities of the plane than a single flight.

Assessment

1. Group work on data collection sheets
2. Observation of student groups
3. Journal questions:
    (a) Explain how you collected your data and what you discovered.
    (b) Why is it necessary to perform multiple trials and then use the average?

Lucky Lindy (page 1)

Team Trials

Trial Number	Distance Traveled (in meters)
1	
2	
3	
4	
5	
6	
7	
8	
9	
10	
Average	

How does taking the average make your results more accurate or typical?

_____

_____

_____

_____

_____

Lucky Lindy (page 2)

Directions: Today you will be working in teams of four. Each of you will design a paper airplane and determine the best design for the team, using the individual flight data you will collect for this sheet. Take turns assuming the following roles: (1) the pilot, (2) the measurement engineer, and (3) the data recorder. Once you have found the best plane, you will need to take 10 trials flying your team plane. Record the data on the Team Trials sheet. This data will be used to determine the class winner. When you have completed the experiment, be sure to answer all of the questions for this activity and be prepared to share your data and ideas with the rest of the teams.

Student	Trial Number	Distance Traveled (in meters)
	1	
	2	
	3	
	Average	

Student	Trial Number	Distance Traveled (in meters)
	1	
	2	
	3	
	Average	

Student	Trial Number	Distance Traveled (in meters)
	1	
	2	
	3	
	Average	

Student	Trial Number	Distance Traveled (in meters)
	1	
	2	
	3	
	Average	

Lucky Lindy (page 3)

Group Analysis

Trial Number	Distance Traveled (in meters)
1	
2	
3	
4	
5	
6	
7	
8	
9	
10	
Average	

June Celebrations

Introduction

June begins on a somber note commemorating the American forces' landing in Europe during World War II, the Normandy Beach invasion. History records that 9,500 Americans are buried in the cemetery in Normandy. Can we even imagine how many people this is? Students will gain some understanding of the number by lining up side by side and measuring how many meters long the line they form is. Using a map, they will see how far the line would extend if there were 9,500 of them on the line.

Flag Day is celebrated on June 14. For our celebration, Symmetry in Flags has students examine six flags of countries in Central America to find the lines and points of symmetry. The students also have an opportunity to be creative; they design their own flag and perhaps even invent their own country to go with the flag.

June 15 is Hug Day—the day for all those people who really need a hug. Our celebration, The World Needs a Hug Today, asks students to determine how many of them it would take to circum-hug the world, a distance of 40,000 kilometers.

If school ends for you in June, then Go Take a Hike! is a wonderful way to say good-bye to your students. Now that they have calculated how many of them it would take to hug the earth, why not estimate how many strides it would take to walk the same distance? In June, when the weather is appealing, take your students outdoors to stride around the earth in celebration of the closing of school.

Normandy Beach Invasion—D Day

Teacher Page

Areas of study

ratio and proportion, large numbers, metric linear measurement, metric weight, area of circles

Concepts

Students will

- use ratio and proportion to solve problems
- understand the magnitude of this historical event in terms of the numbers of casualties
- make the connections between distances in this problem and distances on a map
- compute square miles of a circular area
- understand the weight of a 28-kilogram backpack by actually experiencing it
- work in groups to solve problems

Materials needed

instruments to measure long distances in metric measurements (a trundle wheel works nicely), scales to measure 28 kilograms (approximately 60 pounds), maps to locate cities and/or countries 9,500 people away from where you are located, calculator for each pair of students, backpack and items to total 28 kilograms for each pair of students.

Procedures

Have students line up and hold hands in a straight line. Start at one end of the line and measure to the other end. When the measurement is complete, use the number of students and the distance from the beginning of the line to the end to complete the first fraction in this proportion:

$$\frac{\text{number of students}}{\text{number of meters}} = \frac{9,500}{\text{number of meters}}$$

Have students complete the remainder of the activity, working in pairs. Make calculators available to help with computation.

Assessment

1. Successful completion of activity sheet
2. Observation of student pairs
3. Journal questions:
   (a) Describe how the use of ratio and proportion made solving this problem easier.
   (b) How would the distance have changed if we had 100 more students in our class?

Extension

Have students research the casualties during all of World War II and make the same type of connections (casualties and distance) to understand the magnitude of the bloodshed.

Normandy Beach Invasion—D Day

On June 6, 1944, American forces landed on the beaches of Normandy, France. The purpose was to liberate Europe from Nazi and fascist dictators. Over 5,000 ships and more than 10,000 planes were involved in the attack. When it was all over, 9,500 Americans were dead. A cemetery on the beach memorializes this battle with a cross or a Star of David marking the grave of each of the fallen soldiers.

Directions: Line up side by side with your classmates, holding hands. Your teacher will measure the length of the line. Write the results here: _____ meters. How long would the line be if 9,500 people (the number of Americans who died at Normandy) lined up holding hands? Let's use a ratio and set up a proportion to solve this problem.

$$\frac{\text{number of students}}{\text{number of meters}} = \frac{9,500}{\text{number of meters}}$$

Use this space to compute the length of a line of 9,500 people in meters.

- Use a map to find a city that is 9,500 "people meters" away. It may be easier to convert meters to kilometers. Remember that 1,000 meters is equal to 1 kilometer. _____

- If the 9,500 people length were the radius of a circle, how many square miles would be in this circle. ($A=\pi r^2$) _____

- Each soldier had a pack that weighed about 28 kilograms. Put together a pack weighing this amount. Could you carry this weight? _____

 Multicultural Math Fun: Holidays Around the Year

Symmetry in Flags

Teacher Page

Areas of study

symmetry, problem solving, writing in mathematics

Concepts

Students will

- examine flags to find horizontal and vertical lines of symmetry
- find points of symmetry
- design their own flag with both lines and a point of symmetry

Materials needed

Symmetry in Flags worksheets for each student, crayons/markers/colored pencils, mirrors, rulers, scissors

Procedures

Discuss with students what lines and points of symmetry are and how to determine whether something is a line or a point of symmetry. Have students examine the worksheets and, working alone, draw lines or points of symmetry for the flags of Central America. If you wish, have pictures of the actual flags available so students can see the colors.

Give students time to design their own flags. If mirrors are available, suggest that students use them to help find the line of symmetry. To find a point of symmetry, some students find it easier to cut out a copy of their design to facilitate the actual rotation. Many students have a hard time visualizing rotation and need to physically rotate an object to see if the geometric design has a point of symmetry. Have students color their flags.

Assessment

1. Successful completion of worksheet and flag
2. Observation of students
3. Journal question: Why do you think most flags have lines and points of symmetry built into their design?

Extension

1. If you wish to make this an interdisciplinary project, have students design their flag for an imaginary country and develop the characteristics and idiosyncrasies of their country.
2. Have students examine the United States flag to determine whether there are any points or lines of symmetry.

Symmetry in Flags (page 1)

1. Antigua

4. Honduras

2. Barbados

5. Jamaica

3. Haiti

6. Panama

These flags have been printed in black and white to make it easier to find their symmetry. There are lines of symmetry (either horizontal or vertical) and points of symmetry (where designs can be rotated around a point.)

Which of these flags have lines of symmetry? _____
Can you draw where they are? _____

Which of these flags have points of symmetry? _____
How much do the flags need to be rotated to achieve this symmetry? _____

_____

 Multicultural Math Fun: Holidays Around the Year

Symmetry in Flags (page 2)

Directions: In the space below, design your own flag with both lines and points of symmetry. Below the flag, describe the symmetry you have designed.

My description of the symmetry in this flag:

_____

_____

_____

_____

_____

_____

_____

_____

_____

The World Needs a Hug Today

Teacher Page

Areas of study

measurement, data collection and analysis, circumference, averaging, ratio and proportion, large
numbers

Concepts

Students will

- measure the circumference of a circle
- work collaboratively in groups
- find the arithmetic mean
- use ratio and proportion to solve problems

Materials needed

meter tapes or string and metersticks, calculators (if
available), The World Needs a Hug Today sheets for each group of students,
clipboard for each group

Procedures

Students are divided into groups of five; four students form a circle while the
fifth is the measurement engineer. The students rotate so that each member can
perform the measurement engineer's role. Data are recorded and an average
circumference is calculated for each group. Groups enter their averages on the
Class Data sheet, and the class average is computed. This average is used by
the groups to estimate the number of students that would be needed to hug
the world.

Assessment

1. Successful completion of worksheets
2. Observation of student groups
3. Journal question: If we conducted this experiment with a first-grade class,
   how do you think the data would compare?

The World Needs a Hug Today (page 1)

Data Collection

How many students are needed to give the world a hug? In groups of five, you will approximate an answer to this question.

Directions:

1. Four students form a circle by holding hands. Do not stretch; stand comfortably.

2. The fifth student measures the circumference of this circle.

3. Record your measurement on the table below.

4. Now rotate so that a new member does the measurement and the one who measured joins the circle. Continue this until everyone has had a chance to measure the circumference of the group.

5. Enter your group's mean circumference on the Class Data table.

Trial Number	Circumference
1	
2	
3	
4	
5	
Mean	

Multicultural Math Fun: Holidays Around the Year

The World Needs
a Hug Today (page 2)

Class Data

Group Number	Circumference of Hug
1	
2	
3	
4	
5	
6	
Average Size of Hug	

The World Needs a Hug Today (page 3)

Summary

Now we have the information we need to approximate the number of students we would need to hug the world. We need to know that the earth is about 40,000 kilometers or 40,000,000 meters around.

What is the average circumference (or hug) of our groups of four? _____

Directions: Use this information to compute the number of students we would need to give the world a hug. Write your work and thoughts in the space below. Be sure to explain your reasoning.

_____

_____

_____

_____

_____

_____

_____

_____

_____

_____

Go Take a Hike!

Teacher Page

Areas of study

data collection and organization, problem solving, measurement, finding the mean, collaborative learning

Concepts

Students will

- determine the method they will use to find the length of a stride
- connect the scientific method of data collection with mathematics
- use mathematical data to make connections to social studies and map reading
- measure the length of each team member's stride
- work in cooperative groups to collect data
- find the average (mean) length of a stride

Materials needed

Go Take a Hike! worksheet for each group of four, clipboards for ease of data collection, tape measures or metersticks, calculators

Procedures

Have students form groups of four. Read the directions with the students and have them discuss how they might find the length of a normal stride. Students should be encouraged to take multiple steps and divide. For example, if a student took 20 steps, measured that distance, and then divided by 20, there would be a better chance that the step would represent a normal stride.

Tell students to work together and solve the problem. When groups have finished, have them share their solution with the rest of the class.

Assessment

1. Completion of data collection sheet
2. Observation of student groups
3. Journal question: Describe how your group decided what was necessary to get an accurate measurement of the length of a stride. Why couldn't you just measure one step?

Go Take a Hike!

Suppose you went on a long hike . . . around the circumference of the earth. How many strides would it take? We first need to determine the size of an average stride. Working in groups, we will attempt to find an answer to the question, How big is your stride?

Directions: In your groups, determine what you think a stride is. Then measure the length of a stride for each member of your group and enter these measurements on the table below. Find the mean (or average) length of one stride for the members of your group. But first, in the space provided below, describe what you did to answer the question, What is a stride?

_____

_____

_____

Name of Person	Length of Stride
Mean Length of Stride	

The distance around the earth, at the equator, is about 40,000,000 meters. About how many strides would it take to hike around the world? Use the stride length computed from your group's experiment. _____

_____

July and August Celebrations

Introduction

The summer months can be an exciting time of the year. July begins with an Olympic Games logic problem. Which athlete competes in which sport? An interesting problem for your students! Another activity that revolves around the Olympics, The Top 10 Medal Winners in the 1996 Summer Olympics, introduces your students to matrices, with their rows and columns.

Our national pastime, baseball, is just jam-packed with baseball statistics. An interesting, but seldom seen, statistic is called the slugging percentage. This is a weighted average that takes into account the number of bases achieved when a player gets a hit. Many times the player with the highest batting average does not have the highest slugging percentage. This is a real-world example of percentages to intrigue your students.

On August 14, 1945, President Truman announced the surrender of Japan. To commemorate this date, we honor the Native Americans who kept our secrets a secret, the Navajo Code Talkers. Codes and ciphers have built-in interest for students, so capitalize on this interest with your celebration.

Olympic Games Logic Problem

Directions: Barissa, Beth, Betty, Bob, Barry, and Benny are all Olympic athletes competing in different sports. Use the clues below and the grid to help you figure out which athlete competes in which sport.

	Volleyball	Figure Skating	Basketball	Track	Ice Hockey	Baseball
Barissa						
Beth						
Betty						
Bob						
Barry						
Benny						

Clues:

Betty, Barry, Bob, and Benny play team sports in the Olympic Games.

Bob, Barissa, and Barry run a lot.

Betty and the basketball player jump a lot.

Beth and Benny wear skates to compete.

Bob, Barry, and Betty play with a ball.

The baseball player and Benny use wooden sticks, but in different ways.

Top 10 Medal Winners in 1996 Summer Olympics

Teacher Page

Areas of study

matrices, data analysis, reading charts, computation

Concepts

Students will

- learn about matrices
- analyze the matrix for information
- calculate totals and find weighted totals

Materials needed

Top 10 Medal Winners in 1996 Summer Olympics worksheet for each student, calculators

Procedures

Discuss the matrix with your students. The countries are listed by two criteria: (1) the number of gold medals that they received, and (2) total medals won at these games. For that reason, they are not in order of total medals won. Using the weighted totals, the rank order will change slightly: South Korea won more medals than Cuba or the Ukraine.

Assessment

1. Student products
2. Observation of students
3. Journal questions:
   (a) Design your own 3×3 matrix using the cost of hamburgers, fries, and a soft drink at three fast-food restaurants.
   (b) Ask two questions about your matrix.

Top 10 Medal Winners in 1996 Summer Olympics

Directions: The table below shows the countries that won the most Olympic medals in the 1996 summer Olympic Games held in Atlanta. They are ordered by the number of gold medals they received. Use this information to answer the questions that follow the table.

Country	Gold	Silver	Bronze
United States	44	32	25
Russia	26	21	16
Germany	20	18	27
China	16	22	12
France	15	7	15
Italy	13	10	12
Australia	9	9	23
Cuba	9	8	8
Ukraine	9	2	12
South Korea	7	15	5

Source of Information: *Portland Press Herald,* Monday, August 5, 1996.

1. This is a 10 by 3 matrix because it has 10 rows and 3 columns. The columns represent _____ The rows represent _____

2. Example: (2,3) means go down to the second row and over to the third column. What number is in (2,3)? _____
   What does it stand for? _____

3. In which cell would you find the number of silver medals won by South Korea? _____

4. What was the total number of gold medals won by these 10 countries?

   _____

5. The number 2 appears only once on the matrix. In which cell does it appear? _____
   What does it represent? _____

6. If gold medals are worth 3 points, silver medals worth 2 points, and bronze medals worth 1 point, how many points has each of these countries accumulated?
   United States ____ Russia ____ Germany ____ China ____ France ____
   Italy ____ Australia ____ Cuba ____ Ukraine ____ South Korea ____

Baseball Statistics

Teacher Page

Areas of study

computation, reading a table, percentage, decimals, problem solving, substitution into formulas, ranking data, rounding

Concepts

Students will

- read data from a table
- use formulas to compute percentages
- rank statistics

Materials needed

calculators, Baseball Statistics worksheets for each student

Procedures

Go over the definitions of abbreviations at the top of the table, being sure that all students understand what they mean. Go over the formula, using examples of averages on the tables. Numbers will require rounding to the nearest thousandth.

The difference between batting average (Avg) and slugging percentage is that the latter has a weighted total. Each base earned is counted in the total. For example, a single is multiplied by 1, a double is multiplied by 2, etc. This weighted sum is divided by the number of times at bat (AB) and becomes the slugging percentage.

Assessment

1. Student products
2. Observation of students
3. Journal question: Which player do you believe was the most valuable on the 1989 team? Why?

Extension

Have students calculate the slugging percentages of a local (or their favorite) team using the statistics from a newspaper.

Baseball Statistics (page 1)

The information found on the table below is for players from the 1989 Chicago Cubs. The column headings stand for:

1. Avg is batting average.
2. OBA is on-base average; this differs because walks are counted in this statistic.
3. AB is the number of times the player has been at bat.
4. R is the number of runs.
5. H is the number of hits (singles + doubles + triples + home runs).
6. 2B is the number of doubles.
7. 3B is the number of triples.
8. HR is the number of home runs.
9. RBI is the number of runs batted in.

Batter	Avg	OBA	AB	R	H	1B	2B	3B	HR	RBI
Grace	.311	.396	383	51	119		22	1	12	60
Walton	.309	.347	366	49	113		22	3	5	40
Smith	.299	.355	264	39	79		19	3	7	40
Sandberg	.279	.345	463	78	129		18	4	24	60
Dunston	.274	.324	351	45	96		14	5	8	43
Berryhill	.257	.291	334	37	86		13	0	5	41
Webster	.255	.329	247	35	63		10	3	3	18
Dawson	.245	.298	290	41	71		11	5	14	49
Law	.237	.288	350	32	83		20	2	5	35

The average (batting average) is computed by using the following formula:

$$\text{Average} = \frac{\text{H}}{\text{AB}}$$

Another formula used to tell how well someone bats is called the slugging percentage; this percentage indicates the total number of bases earned. This is a weighted percentage. To find the slugging percentage, use this formula:

$$\text{Slugging percentage} = \frac{(1B \times 1) + (2B \times 2) + (3B \times 3) + (HR \times 4)}{AB}$$

Directions: Since the table does not indicate total number of 1B's, calculate those by adding together the doubles, triples, and home runs and subtracting this sum from the total number of hits. For example: Dawson got 71 total number of hits. The sum of his 2B's, 3B's, and HR's is 30; 71 – 30 = 41. Dawson got 41 singles. Now fill in the 1B column in the table.

Multicultural Math Fun: Holidays Around the Year

Baseball Statistics (page 2)

Directions: Use the table you have just completed to compute the slugging percentages for the players.

Batter	Slugging Percentage	Batting Average
Grace		.311
Walton		.309
Smith		.299
Sandberg		.279
Dunston		.274
Berryhill		.257
Webster		.255
Dawson		.245
Law		.237

How do the slugging percentages compare with the batting averages?

_____

_____

Directions: Using slugging percentages, rank the players in the blank table below.

Batter	Slugging Percentage	Batting Average

Navajo Code Talkers

Teacher Page

Areas of study
  problem solving, decoding and encoding, patterns

Concepts
  Students will
  - examine a variety of codes and look for patterns
  - decode and encode statements
  - make mathematical connections
  - develop their own codes

Materials needed
  "Navajo Code Talkers" worksheets for each student, reference books for additional experiences with codes

Procedures
  Before beginning this activity, ask students if they are familiar with any codes and ciphers. Allow them time to discuss the need to conceal communication. Discuss the difference between codes and ciphers: A code replaces a word with a new word or symbol; a cipher replaces each letter with a symbol.

  Explain the important role the Navajos played during World War II in protecting American secrets. Before they began their work, it was impossible to keep the Japanese from intercepting and decoding our secret messages, and so every move Americans made was known. Because the Navajo nation language is so difficult to understand, Navajo Code Talkers spoke to each other without fear of being understood.

Assessment
  1. Student performance on the code sheet
  2. Journal entry: Develop your own code or cipher. Write a key and encode a message for your classmates to solve.

Extension
  - Have students develop additional codes and ciphers.
  - Have students research the role of the Navajo Code Talkers.
  - Have students research the unique language and customs of the Navajo nation.

Navajo Code Talkers (page 1)

During World War II, Navajo Code Talkers played an important role in protecting American secrets in the Pacific. While the Japanese could crack most codes, they could not understand the Navajo messages. These codes were developed from the extraordinarily complex languages of the Navajo nation, which are based on tone and inflection as well as vocabulary. Navajo Code Talkers participated in key battles on Saipan, Guadalcanal, and Iwo Jima. Because of these brave men, American soldiers were able to communicate secret messages without fear they would be understood by the Japanese. In honor of these brave men, let's study some codes and ciphers.

Codes and ciphers are used to conceal a communication. A code replaces a word with a new word or symbol; a cipher replaces each letter with a symbol. Let's examine two secret codes. One substitutes numbers for each letter. The other, called the pigpen code, substitutes a symbol for each letter.

Number Code

The letters of the alphabet are placed in a 5 × 5 grid; I and J are placed in the same box because they are never interchangeable in a word. The key identifies each letter with the number of its row and the number of its column. For example, 43 is S and 34 is O.

	1	2	3	4	5
1	A	B	C	D	E
2	F	G	H	I/J	K
3	L	M	N	O	P
4	Q	R	S	T	U
5	V	W	X	Y	Z

Try to decipher this code:

44 23 15   33 11 51 11 24 34   13 34 14 15   44 11 31 25 15 42 43   52 15 42 15
12 42 11 51 15   11 33 14   31 34 54 11 31   11 32 15 42 24 13 11 33 43.

Now encode this message:
Education holds the keys to success.

Navajo Code Talkers (page 2)

Key

A	B	C	D	E	F	G	H	I	J	K	L	M
11	12	13	14	15	21	22	23	24	24	25	31	32

N	O	P	Q	R	S	T	U	V	W	X	Y	Z
33	34	35	41	42	43	44	45	51	52	53	54	55

Squares and Crosses

This next code is called the old pigpen and was used over 100 years ago during the Civil War. The four figures make up 26 spaces, one for each letter of the alphabet. Dots under one half of the letters allow the same shape to be used for two different letters.

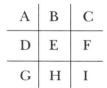 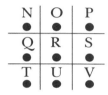

Try to decipher this code:

Answer Key

Fanya Montalvo (page 2)

1. 3.6 words per second
2. 648,000 words per minute; 10,800 words per second
3. 119,500 hours; 4,979 days

Mary Somerville (page 3)

1. 2,390 hours
2. your weight × 0.17
3. $25,840,000,000
4. Answers will vary.
5. 50 pounds

Logical Mystery 1 (page 4)

Rodriguez: house on left; poodle

McCarthy: middle house; no dog

Hester: house on right; Labrador retriever

Logical Mystery 2 (page 5)

The smallest number of passes is five if all of the rules are followed.

Marvin	Mabel	Mickey
M	S	L
M, L	S	O
M, L	O	S
M	O	S, L
O	M	S, L
L	M	S

A Matrix Mystery (page 6)

	Doctor	Lawyer	Architect
Maria	X	Lawyer	X
Julia	X	X	Architect
Olga	Doctor	X	X

Halloween Costumes (page 27)

$3 \times 4 \times 3 = 36$

A Halloween Problem (page 28)

witch legs: $13 \times 2 = 26$

cat legs: $13 \times 7 \times 7 \times 4 = 2,548$

kitten legs: $13 \times 7 \times 7 \times 7 \times 4 = 17,836$

$26 + 2,548 + 17,836 = 20,410$

How Many Americans Vote? (page 31)

State	1984 %	1988 %	% ±	State	1984 %	1988 %	% ±	State	1984 %	1988 %	% ±
Ala.	50	46	–8	Ky.	51	48	–6	N. Dak.	63	62	–2
Alaska	59	52	–12	La.	55	51	–7	Ohio	58	55	–5
Ariz.	45	45	0	Maine	65	62	–5	Okla.	52	48	–8
Ark.	52	47	–10	Md.	51	49	–4	Oreg.	62	59	–5
Calif.	50	47	–6	Mass.	58	58	0	Pa.	54	50	–7
Colo.	55	55	0	Mich.	58	54	–7	R.I.	56	53	–5
Conn.	61	58	–5	Minn.	68	66	–3	S.C.	41	39	–5
Del.	55	51	–7	Miss.	52	51	–2	S. Dak.	63	61	–3
D.C.	43	39	–9	Mo.	57	55	–4	Tenn.	49	45	–8
Fla.	48	45	–6	Mont.	65	62	–5	Tex.	47	44	–6
Ga.	42	39	–7	Nebr.	56	57	+2	Utah	62	60	–3
Hawaii	44	43	–2	Nev.	41	45	+10	Vt.	60	59	–2
Idaho	60	58	–3	N.H.	53	55	+4	Va.	51	48	–6
Ill.	57	53	–7	N.J.	57	52	–9	Wash.	58	55	–5
Ind.	57	53	–7	N. Mex.	51	47	–8	W.Va.	52	47	–10
Iowa	62	60	–3	N.Y.	51	48	–6	Wis.	63	62	–2
Kans.	56	54	–4	N.C.	47	43	–9	Wyo.	53	50	–6

1. Holiday Gifts (page 51)

S = 2 John

N = 2(2 John) + 1

Jill = 2(2 John) + 1 – 2

$$J + 2J + 2(2J) + 1 + 2(2J) + 1 – 2 = 22$$
$$\underbrace{\qquad}_{4J} \qquad \underbrace{\qquad}_{4J}$$

John: 2

Sam: 4

Noel: 9

Jill: $\underline{7}$

22

2. Santa's Trip (page 51)

Santa must travel right three times and up three times to get to Your House. The number of paths is how many different ways you can travel Right and Up.

R = move to right one block
U = move up one block
The paths are

1. RRRUUU	11. UUURRR
2. RRURUU	12. UURURR
3. RRUURU	13. UURRUR
4. RRUUUR	14. UURRRU
5. RURRUU	15. URUUUR
6. RURURU	16. URURUR
7. RURUUR	17. URURRU
8. RUURRU	18. URRUUR
9. RUURUR	19. URRURU
10. RUUURR	20. URRRUR

3. Gifts Galore (page 51)

The answer is 61. If Lisa had 1 sibling, the gifts would be divided between two people and Lisa would receive one more than her sibling. The number of gifts would be a multiple of 2 plus 1. If Lisa had 2 siblings, the gifts would be divided among three children. The number of gifts would be a multiple of 3 plus 1. If Lisa had 3 siblings, the number of gifts would be a multiple of 4 plus 1. If Lisa had 4 siblings, the number of gifts would be a multiple of 5 plus 1. If Lisa had 5 siblings, the number of gifts would be a multiple of 6 plus 1.

$61 \div 2 = 30 \text{ r } 1$
$61 \div 3 = 20 \text{ r } 1$
$61 \div 4 = 15 \text{ r } 1$
$61 \div 5 = 12 \text{ r } 1$
$61 \div 6 = 10 \text{ r } 1$

The number of gifts purchased would be the Least Common Multiple $\{2,3,4,5,6\} + 1$. The LCM of $\{2,3,4,5,6\}$ is $2^2 \times 3 \times 5$ or 60. The number of gifts purchased is 61.

Z-Day (page 54)

1. Zaire
2. zero
3. zilch
4. Zambia
5. Zuni

Shamrocks and Bunnies (page 103)

three (. . . papa bunny left one leaf on three shamrocks.)

April Fool's Mathematics Test (page 105)

1. The person slept for only one hour unless he or she remembered to set the alarm for A.M. time.

2. Their calendar does, in fact, have a fourth day in the month of July.

3. The average person has only one birthday, as this represents the day the person was born.

4. Why would you bury a living person?

5. Wouldn't you need to light the match first?

6. Every month has 28 days.

7. The pills would last for only one hour; you take one immediately, one a half hour later, and the last one, an hour later than the first.

8. The dog can only run halfway into the forest; after that the dog would be running out of the forest.

9. 70. When you divide 30 by $\frac{1}{2}$ ($30 \div \frac{1}{2}$), the answer is 60 and $60 + 10 = 70$.

10. You can't remove dirt from a hole; by definition it's empty!

Using Five 5's (page 110)

$$(5 + 5) \div 5 - \frac{5}{5} = 1$$

$$(5 + 5) \div 5 + (5 - 5) = 2$$

$$(5 + 5) \div 5 + \frac{5}{5} = 3$$

$$\frac{5 + 5 + 5 + 5}{5} = 4$$

$$\frac{5}{5} \times 5 + (5 - 5) = 5$$

$$\frac{5}{5} + 5 + (5 - 5) = 6$$

$$\frac{5}{5} + \frac{5}{5} + 5 = 7$$

$$(5 + 5 + 5) \div 5 + 5 = 8$$

$$\frac{(5 \times 5) - 5}{5} + 5 = 9$$

$$5 + 5 - [(5 - 5) \times 5] = 10$$

Population of Mexico's Cities (page 112)

Major Cities	Population	Percent of Population
Mexico City	20,207,000	22.9
Guadalajara	3,262,000	3.7
Monterrey	2,837,000	3.2
Puebla	836,000	.9
León	656,000	.7
Ciudad Juarez	567,000	.6
Culiacán	560,000	.6
Mexicali	511,000	.6
Tijuana	461,000	.5
Mérida	425,000	.5
Acapulco	409,000	.5
Chihuahua	407,000	.5
San Luis Potosí	407,000	.5
Hermosillo	341,000	.4
Mazatlán	250,000	.3

Temperature Highs and Lows (page 115)

Place	Temperature in ° Celsius	Temperature in ° Fahrenheit
Death Valley, California	57° C	134.6
Tirat Tsvi, Israel	54° C	129.2
Seville, Spain	50° C	122
Vostok, Antarctica	–89° C	–128.2
Snag, Yukon	–63° C	–81.4
Ilfrane, Morocco	–24° C	–11.2

The Highest and Coldest Mountains (page 116)

Highest Mountain by Continent				
Continent	Location	Name of Mountain	Height (in feet)	Temperature at the Top
North America	Alaska	Mount McKinley	20,320	0°
South America	Argentina	Mount Aconcagua	22,834	−8°
Africa	Tanzania	Mount Kilimanjaro	19,340	+4°
Asia	Nepal/Tibet	Mount Everest	29,028	−29°
Eastern Europe	Russia	Mount Eibrus	18,510	+6°
Western Europe	France	Mont Blanc	15,771	+15°
Antarctica	Ellsworth Land	Vinson Massif	16,864	+12°
Oceania	New Zealand	Mount Cook	12,349	+27°

Olympic Games Logic Problem (page 134)

	Volleyball	Figure Skating	Basketball	Track	Ice Hockey	Baseball
Barissa				■		
Beth		■				
Betty	■					
Bob			■			
Barry						■
Benny					■	

Top 10 Medal Winners in the 1996 Summer Olympics (page 136)

1. medals; countries

2. 16; the number of bronze medals received by Russia

3. (10, 2)

4. 168

5. (9, 2)

6. United States: 221
   Russia: 136
   Germany: 123
   China: 104
   France: 74
   Italy: 71
   Australia: 68
   Cuba: 51
   Ukraine: 43
   South Korea: 56

Baseball Statistics (page 138)

Batter	Avg	OBA	AB	R	H	1B	2B	3B	HR	RBI
Grace	.311	.396	383	51	119	84	22	1	12	60
Walton	.309	.347	366	49	113	83	22	3	5	40
Smith	.299	.355	264	39	79	50	19	3	7	40
Sandberg	.279	.345	463	78	129	83	18	4	24	60
Dunston	.274	.324	351	45	96	69	14	5	8	43
Berryhill	.257	.291	334	37	86	68	13	0	5	41
Webster	.255	.329	247	35	63	47	10	3	3	18
Dawson	.245	.298	290	41	71	41	11	5	14	49
Law	.237	.288	350	32	83	56	20	2	5	35

Baseball Statistics (page 139)

Batter	Slugging Percentage	Batting Average
Grace 179/383	.467	.311
Walton 156/366	.426	.309
Smith 125/264	.473	.299
Sandberg 227/463	.490	.279
Dunston 144/351	.410	.274
Berryhill 114/334	.341	.257
Webster 88/247	.356	.255
Dawson 134/290	.462	.245
Law 122/350	.349	.237

Batter	Slugging Percentage	Batting Average
Sandberg	.490	.279
Smith	.473	.299
Grace	.467	.311
Dawson	.462	.245
Walton	.426	.309
Dunston	.410	.274
Webster	.356	.255
Law	.349	.237
Berryhill	.341	.257

Navajo Code Talkers (page 141)

```
T H E      N A V A J O      C O D E      T A L K E R S      W E R E
44 23 15    33 11 51 11 24 34    13 34 14 15    44 11 31 25 15 42 43    52 15 42 15


B R A V E      A N D      L O Y A L      A M E R I C A N S
12 42 11 51 15    11 33 14    31 34 54 11 31    11 32 15 42 24 13 11 33 43.
```

Education hold the keys to success.
15 14 45 13 11 44 24 34 33   23 34 31 14 43   44 23 15   25 15 54 43   44 34
43 45 13 13 15 43 43

(page 142)

```
I    W I L L    F I G H T    N O    M O R E

F O R E V E R    C H I E F    J O S E P H
```